S0-AQE-473

SOCIETY TO L&D... STAT! STAT! STAT!

MURRAY A. FREEDMAN, MD

SOCIETY TO
L&D...
STAT! STAT! STAT!

MURRAY A. FREEDMAN, MD

**Marshwinds
Publications**

Copyright © 1988 by Murray A. Freedman, M.D.
All rights reserved.

The article "The Doctor Who Chose Death Over a Malpractice Trial," reprinted by permission from the June 22, 1987 issue of Medical Economics. Copyright © 1987 and published by Medical Economics Company, Inc. at Oradell, N.J. 07649.

ISBN 0-9614496-1-6

Library of Congress Catalog Card No. 88-62504

Printed in the United States of America

DEDICATION

This book is dedicated to my patients: past, present, and future. I have stated repeatedly that I wanted my epitaph to read: "thanks to my patients for making my life so gratifying and necessary." It is truly a delight to care for 95% of the patients in one's practice. There will always be that other 5%. Let us not have life's joy or beauty spoiled by a small fraction of the whole. This should be true whether we are referring to patients, physicians, attorneys or simply apples. Perhaps we can weed out those who are out of sync and thereby preserve life's pleasures.

ACKNOWLEDGMENTS

There are many people who have contributed to this book. By not being specific in my thanks, I am attempting to avoid overlooking anyone. I hope that I will continue to thank you personally and there is no doubt in my mind that you are aware of my sincere gratitude.

I pray that your efforts on my behalf will be rewarded by this book being read by scores of patients and that it will serve society well. What greater appreciation and reparation could there be than to have contributed positively to the health care of millions of Americans? A tremendous collective thank you is definitely in order.

Last, but not least, I owe a special thanks to my family. Preparing a book in one's "spare time" means borrowing personal time from loved ones. Family love and support are what life is really all about, and I am sure Sandra, Stacy, and Allen know how much I love and appreciate them.

CONTENTS

Dedication v
Acknowledgments vii
Foreword xi

CHAPTER 1
  The Liability Crisis 1
CHAPTER 2
  The Joy of Obstetrics 13
CHAPTER 3
  Consumerism: Patients' Expectations 27
CHAPTER 4
  What Malpractice Means to the Physician 45
CHAPTER 5
  Abuse of the Tort Law System 69
CHAPTER 6
  Society's Role in Resolving the Crisis 87

FOREWORD

There is a serious crisis. It is not simply a liability crisis. It is far more serious than malpractice and negligence in medicine. It is even more serious than the injustices and inequities in the present tort law system.

The true crisis is the quality of your health care in the near future. Not only is the interest in medical careers waning, but also the quality of applicants in the health care industry is plummeting. Medical authorities unanimously agree that the declining appeal of medical careers requires immediate attention.

Three factors are most prevalent in discouraging potential health care providers: AIDS, big "for-profit" business, and the liability issue. No imminent solution to AIDS is on the horizon. Large businesses recognize the potential profitability in the health care industry, and their interest will only increase with time. Furthermore, cost containment and tight budgets will continue to haunt most government funded programs.

The third factor, malpractice and the liability crisis, is the one ominous factor upon which we can have a positive impact. It can be done immediately and rather simply.

After reading this book, you will agree that several simple changes SHOULD be instituted. You, the patient, will benefit immediately since reparation for injury will be made equitable rather than resemble a lottery system. You, society, will benefit because these changes will enable the United States to continue to enjoy the finest medical care system in the world.

CHAPTER 1

The Liability Crisis

IT IS 4 A.M. I have a terrible pain in my abdomen. Is it labor? I don't think so, but the pain is getting worse. Is the baby alive? Please move a little, baby. Kick and let me know you are still alive. Will this pain kill us both? There is no doubt now: something is terribly wrong.

The clock reads 4:10 A.M. I am bleeeding now. Maybe the baby is dying and that is why I hurt. My God, I think we are both going to die. I need my doctor. I need help.

It is 4:20 A.M. I'll call my new obstetrician. He'll assure me things are O.K. It hurts. I'm terribly frightened. Why did all the local obstetricians stop delivering babies? My obstetrician is now in a town 60 miles away, but surely I can last long enough to get there. Please kick again, baby. The pain's worse . . . and so is the bleeding. I'm scared. I know my doctor will help me—even though the whole world is asleep, surely he will help me.

Oh Lord, sheer panic: my obstetrician has gone to a meeting. He is not even available this week. He is attending one of those malpractice seminars trying to learn how to defend himself in court. Who will help me? Could a nurse take care of me? I've come too far to let this baby die. I need a doctor. When I got married, I wanted the very best obstetrician in the world to deliver my baby. When I got pregnant, I wanted my obstetrician to deliver my baby. Now I just want *an* obstetrician to deliver my baby. There are so few doctors practicing obstetrics these days. Why is it so hard to find an obstetrician?

IT IS 4 A.M. I cannot get back to sleep again this time. That phone call from Ms. Jones about her cold could easily have waited until morning. "Could breathing through my mouth all night harm my baby?" That may qualify as the most unnecessary phone call of the month. It's free,

1

it makes her feel better, and the phone is very convenient. Besides, I did not even have to think very hard. My goodness, I should be happy. I have not had to get out of bed all night long! What a blessing: only two phone calls after 11 P.M. I should be extremely grateful.

But how can I be grateful? I'm angry. Come to think of it, I'm furious. I will be in court in a couple of weeks. This has been going on now for over two years. Definitely the worst two years of my life. Every phone call or other waking event is followed by this same agitation and insomnia.

I'm hostile enough to have a stroke! He and his wife are suing me because they have a retarded child. I didn't cause it—I just delivered the child for them. 4 A.M. Another 4 A.M., only it was Thanksgiving. What a misnomer for that particular Thursday.

I am absolutely sure that the infant was retarded long before labor even began. She drank excessively, smoked incessantly (pot included), and frequently used "hard" drugs. She didn't even want to be pregnant, and they had both had venereal diseases on at least two occasions that I treated her. Her terrible personal health maintenance and abuse of over-the-counter medications in early pregnancy are more likely to have caused her harm than the delivery. These facts won't matter though. Only one fact will be important in court: can I prove that I did not cause her infant to be retarded? All they will see is a beautiful, pathetic, retarded child, helplessly afflicted.

I remember the delivery vividly—even though it was 17 years ago! Normal labor, normal everything—until after the delivery of the head. The shoulders were indeed difficult to deliver. How could a normal body have such big shoulders! There is no doubt that the child's head was small compared with those shoulders. Anyway, it makes no difference now. The point today is that the infant did have some difficulty breathing initially, and I must prove that the mental retardation was not the result of anything I did. I am *guilty* until *proved* innocent. Proving my innocence will be tough, too.

I know that even several minutes without any oxygen at all will not cause an infant's retardation. But a jury won't know that. Decreased oxygen for that brief period might cause some brain damage to an infant previously compromised in some way—but not by itself. Too bad I can't prove that to the jury either. Too bad I can't prove that hundreds, maybe thousands of things, are more likely to have caused this child to have mental retardation than a slightly difficult delivery and a problem with respiration during the first few minutes of life.

That part is history. The jury will know little if any medicine. No human being can possibly teach them enough medicine to understand the many complexities involved. Even several medical experts cannot decide with any degree of certainty how much each factor in her health care might have been involved as to the specific cause and effect of the retardation. A world-famous geneticist strongly believes that this child has a chromosome or inherited defect, and the neurological deficit had nothing to do with events occurring after the day of conception. There will be an opposing "expert," however, who will swear that I ruined this lovely, normal child through my gross negligence, which is so obvious to him. There is a good chance this "expert" is no longer even a practicing physician. He may well be a typical "hired gun."

I am frustrated to think that I am being ransomed for doing a credible job during a delivery. I have paid astronomic malpractice premiums, yet I may now lose everything in spite of that. I actually carry insurance for the said purpose of compensating anyone I may harm, but I could ultimately owe these people millions. I never really thought about making millions—but to owe millions! If your car liability insurance did not cover you for the possible damage done when you wrecked the car, you too might wonder just why you pay premiums if indeed you are not adequately protected.

No wonder my wife has been so irritable. Her security is threatened. Someone is attempting to take everything away from us. We could lose our home, our savings, even my retirement money. She, too, remembers what it was like being $20,000 in debt at the conclusion of my medical training.

"We've worked too hard to be ruined by someone without just cause," she says.

I must admit, I agree. I have to agree with my son, too, even though he ended up with a horrible black eye. All he did was try to defend his father's honor when one of the bullies in his class ridiculed me for "botching" a delivery and ruining a healthy baby. I only hope my elderly parents who live 300 miles away will be spared the degradation of this entire affair.

All any person can do is the best that is humanly possible—and that is exactly what I did for this patient. How bizarre that I can now be stripped entirely of my possessions, though in fact I made absolutely no mistake. I am indeed a victim of circumstance.

Much to my chagrin, I shall become a victim of the press, as well. Media coverage thrives on sensationalism, and some dramatic quotes will provide some juicy headlines. Statements from the "hired gun" might easily include terms of endearment for the defendant doctor such as "negligent," "incompetent," and "unfit to practice." It makes great reading to reproduce "expert" testimony concerning how careless or shoddy treatment destroyed a lovely, healthy child. . . .

I shall suffer abuse. I am prepared for that. But what about all the complacent, insensitive, incompetent doctors? The majority of the "bad guys" commit malpractice, and it goes unrecognized. Most local physicians know who the better doctors in a community are—and, more important, who the sorry ones are. Sadly enough, under the present system of medical jurisprudence, the truly incompetent doctor is allowed to walk away relatively unscathed from most liability suits. If the suit doesn't exceed his liability coverage, the insurance company simply picks up the tab. What is sorely needed is a panel made up in part of true medical experts who can evaluate claims quickly and simply and then pay deserving, injured parties according to predetermined guidelines for specific injury. An additional benefit of such a panel would be its ability to distinguish readily the physician who simply encounters an imperfect result from the one who is truly negligent. What a logical trade-off: have doctors evaluate other doctors and medicine, and have lawyers stick to strictly legal matters. Medicine is both an art and a science, and as such it does not lend itself to legal definitions.

Not everyone will welcome such an arbitration panel made up of unbiased professionals. After all, the plaintiff is being used to generate a tremendous amount of money for the legal profession. The plaintiff receives less than one-third of the money in the whole process. Over two-thirds is usurped by the legal community, primarily by defense and plaintiff attorneys. Under the present medical liability system, we take a "malresult" and then work backward to see if someone can make big bucks from it. It is not unlike a lottery: Let me see if my injury can lead to a windfall judgment while the legal profession officiates over the process. I suppose I am just being naïve . . . I thought the basic principle was to address bad medicine and equitably compensate injured patients.

I am becoming extremely angry again. I can just imagine the patient's lawyer thinking that if he can get a $6-million settlement, he will make a cool, quick $2 million—$2 million for his contribution, however little that may be. At an hourly rate, this might easily equate to $5,000 to $10,000 per hour in many cases. Not bad pay, huh? If the suit is a clear-cut case of an error in the course of treatment, it might be settled out of court quickly and quietly. In such a case, the plaintiff's attorney might be making in excess of $100,000 per hour, since so little time would be required. I can understand their advertising now, hoping to find that rainbow. I would like to think, though, that in such a case, the injured party would receive at least 90 percent of the settlement.

Besides vividly remembering the delivery, I also remember my lawyer's first impression of the case shortly after it was filed two years ago. He recommended settling quietly. He made reference to a similar suit wherein the baby's shoulders were stuck, the infant suffered some brain damage, and the award was in excess of $9 million. I became ill, my knees were weak. My malpractice coverage was for $1 million. That would leave me only $8 million short! Two other comments my counselor made during our initial discussion alarmed me.

"Don't take it personally," he said.

Of course not. You have just been ruthlessly humiliated by an accusation of medical malpractice for allegedly causing brain damage to a beautiful, healthy infant, but do not take it personally. That left me speechless and a little short of breath.

He then asked me whether the baby had lived, and he was disappointed that the infant had survived. He explained his callous attitude: Jury settlements are greatly influenced by emotion, and the sympathy engendered by the physical presence of a pathetic, retarded child can

5

be extremely profound. As he put it, live babies bring much more in court than dead ones.

Once again, I was speechless. Can the world be so cruel?

I am very tired, but my anxiety keeps me from falling asleep. I wonder if any other business or profession operates under an insurance system that allows its properly insured personnel to be so exposed to ruin. Would businessmen, politicians, judges, or teachers perform their daily duties knowing that a decision—any single decision—could totally destroy them? It doesn't even have to be the wrong decision. Who would risk his or her entire pension on such a daily basis?

This whole ordeal has been a total disaster. I tried for weeks to find descriptive terminology to explain my feelings. Anger, fear, betrayal, grief, apprehension, despair, loneliness, sadness, irritability, dejection—all of these fit, but the word which best typifies the feeling is devastation. Webster defines "devastate" as "bring to ruin or desolation . . . to reduce to chaos or disorder; synonym, see ravage." How devastating!

I must get some sleep. I am operating this morning, and a lady and her baby's life are depending on me. I cannot allow one angry patient and a couple of "hungry" professionals to ruin an otherwise unblemished, rewarding career.

This anxiety is getting to be unbearable. I am not sure I can continue to practice obstetrics. The stress of each delivery and the potential sacrifice that my family and I will have to make if the outcome is not perfect are just *too* great. The anxiety exceeds the joy. Maybe the public will get involved before it is too late. The interest in medical careers has diminished dramatically. A decline in the quality of medical care will soon follow. I wonder how many other physicians realize how dreadfully vulnerable we are and how unfair the present system of medical jurisprudence is. If physicians do realize this, then how can we educate the public? After all, in the final analysis, it is their own personal medical care that is in jeopardy.

These two vignettes are purely hypothetical. They could, however, be very real in view of the ever-expanding liability crisis in medicine to-

6

day. This crisis is most prevalent in obstetrics, but it is rapidly permeating all medical specialities.

The purpose of this book is twofold. The first goal is to explain to my former obstetrical patients why I felt compelled to discontinue the practice of obstetrics (OB). Since over 40 percent of my fellow obstetricians in the state of Georgia are either in the process of stopping or have already stopped their OB practice, obviously a rather serious problem exists now. Women may soon find it extremely difficult to obtain good obstetrical care if this trend continues.

Why have so many phyicians stopped OB? It is not the economics of malpractice in obstetrics, though this certainly cannot be ignored. More important, it is the stress that exists because of the litigious attitude of patients and attorneys irrespective of the quality of medical care. The anxiety is constant and inescapable.

The second goal in writing this book is a sincere desire to educate the public to the fact that the inacessibility of medical care will not be limited to obstetrics. Your own personal health care is truly in jeopardy. Obstetrics just happens to be the specialty most affected by this crisis. As was seen recently in Florida, the nonavailability of neurosurgeons for head injuries reached dangerous proportions when it was almost impossible to find care for accident victims. Because of such an oppressive liability problem, South Florida emergency room doctors literally went "on strike" to focus public attention on the crisis. As you will see in this book, such a callous approach is out of character for physicians—but a crisis exists and something must be done.

Six out of every ten physicians have been sued; one of every three obstetricians is currently being sued. Almost every single neurosurgeon in Florida has been sued at least once, and many, numerous times. The current system of awarding damages in malpractice suits resembles a lottery system rather than an equitable system compensating deserving individuals. Even with the large sums awarded in some malpractice cases, you will be astounded to learn that victims of malpractice receive only 28 cents of each dollar paid to the malpractice insurance carriers; the vast majority of the money is going to the legal profession.[1]

There is some awfully poor and unacceptable medicine being practiced in this country. There is no doubt about it. The majority of physicians strongly favor implementing a mechanism to correct this, but the present tort law system does precious little, if anything, to address the quality of medical care. The present system of medical jurisprudence begs revision. An ever-increasing number of doctors are finding the present system intolerable. Once you know the facts, you will agree: your very health is at stake.

You will undoubtedly be frightened to learn that the quality of medical care in the United States may decline drastically very soon. The number of applicants to medical school has decreased from over 5 applicants per position in the mid-1970s to fewer than 1½ per position in 1987. The AIDS virus and interference of "big business" or for-profit organizations have had a distinct, adverse effect on the appeal of medical careers—but not nearly so much as the liability problem. The malpractice crisis has become the principal focus of the national OB-GYN organization in 1988, and rightfully so. This is not just another story of crying wolf. You yourself could well have difficulty finding a good doctor in the near future—especially an obstetrician.

Medicine is changing; society is changing; society is changing medicine. "Where have all the OB's gone?" may well become the theme song of the early 1990s.

The personal anguish of the obstetrician is revealed in the chapters that follow, beginning with delightful past experiences and contrasting them to the present disenchantment. Obstetrics has become an anxiety-laden medical specialty, too much influenced by consumer advocate dominance. Will the unpleasantries lead the majority of obstetricians to deny themselves the exhilarating experience of "birthing babies"? A generation ago, physicians and health care professionals encouraged "their own" to pursue similar careers. Today, these professionals are actually discouraging their children from seeking medical careers. An attitude prevalent among many young physicians today is that they can hardly await the day when they are able to discontinue the practice of medicine; yet so many older physicians relish the very thought of continuing to practice as long as possible. This is a sad testimonial to the future of medicine—especially for obstetrics.

8

The Liability Crisis

For 15 years, delivering babies had remained the most exciting event in my life. This was not just an occasional joy; it was a constant and repetitve "high." I can honestly say that, even now, nothing is as exhilarating as a delivery—be it a vaginal delivery or a Caesarean delivery. But by the same token, nothing is as much of a relief when it is over and all goes well. You see, the *blessed event* is now overshadowed by anxiety and the fear of anything less than a perfect outcome. And it makes very little difference that the infant is normal just at birth because at any time during the next 20 years the physician's liability persists!*

In 1986, 12 percent of the obstetricians in the United States had discontinued delivering babies. This year (1988) that figure will probably increase to 20 percent. In several states, this figure is already in excess of 40 percent! This crisis—an inaccessibility of good obstetrical care —is because the scale of justice is weighted against the practicing obstetrician. Significant factors contributing to this alarming discontinuation of obstetrical practice include:

1. **High malpractice premiums.** Obstetricians pay the second highest malpractice premiums in medicine today (second only to neurosurgeons). This premium is currently $59,000 per year per physician practicing obstetrics in the state of Georgia. In some states, this yearly malpractice premium is in excess of $200,000, thereby making it prohibitive for some physicians to enter private practice after completing their extensive training process.
2. **Frequency of malpractice suits.** Seven out of every 10 obstetricians have been sued at least once. A 35-year career in obstetrics carries with it an average of 8 suits, and each suit requires 2 to 5 years to settle.
3. **Extended statute of limitations.** Obstetrics has the most extended statute of limitations of any branch of medicine. The

---

*The statute of limitations in Georgia was amended in 1987 to include the standard 2-year liability and only 5 additional years for infants rather than the 18 years as previously legislated. The liability for an impaired infant born in 1987, however, will still persist for 19 years (that is, through 2006!).

normal 2-year statute has an additional 18-year liability until the child reaches adulthood.
4. **Responsibility has replaced accountability for injury.** Obstetricians are often sued for "damages" that may well have antedated the alleged incident. The classic example is that of the compromised infant wherein the injury actually occurred before labor. The obstetrican is held responsible for the impaired infant even though he did not *cause* the impairment.

Is it any wonder that I developed a personal aphorism: "If you are lucky, the best you can do is play for a 'tie.' " " If everything goes smoothly and both mother and infant are healthy (that is, a "tie"), then all is well and good. If mother or infant is in any way compromised, you *lose* even though it is through no fault of your own. Anything less than a perfect outcome elicits the instantaneous fear of legal repercussions. Enormous settlements in numerous medical malpractice suits —many of which were awarded *in spite of* good care—have left physicians in a rather untenable position. If providing good quality care is not an adequate defense against malpractice claims, the "game" is not being played fairly. Thus, the increasing exodus from obstetrics.

The metamorphosis from joy to fear has been a rather painful one for me. Obstetricians are "softies." I still get a lump in my throat when I hear the national anthem. I get tears in my eyes every time my son scores a soccer goal. I beamed with pride, almost cried, when I played tennis with my daughter and we won, qualifying to play in the "Nationals" in the Equitable Family Challenge as a part of the U.S. Open Tennis Championships in New York in 1986. Obstetricians are basically sensitive, caring, *good* people. We like our patients, and we love our work—if we didn't, would we have chosen a specialty with so much night work and weekend commitment? Few if any other medical specialties operate on such a full 24-hour-per-day schedule by their own choice. And yet, at this point, the very best we can do is attempt to "tie."

You must be the judge. If changes are necessary, you must help us make them. The changes will not be *legislated* because too many lawyers are receiving tremendous sums of money under the current system. Only you, our patients, can alter the present injustices. Just as you needed your chosen obstetrician at the "appointed" hour, it is now *you* who is needed.

NOTES

1. Pearse, W. H., Professional Liability: Epidemiology and Demography, Clin. Obstet. Gynecol. 1988, 31:148.

CHAPTER 2

The Joy of Obstetrics

HAVING A BABY may just be the single most exciting event in one's life. This may be true not only for the mother, father, and the family but also perhaps for the *obstetrician,* as well. Most women reflect upon their pregnancy as a most rewarding experience. There may be some minor illnesses or inconveniences, but the vast majority of women (and usually their spouses) reflect upon the pregnancy with pleasant memories. After all, what can be more exciting than life itself! What may be a little surprising to you, though, is that the obstetrician readily identifies with this process, too.

You see, we obstetricians feel very much a part of this team effort. We become attached just as you do. If anyone doubts this strong bond of friendship and respect, ask an obstetrician about his personal feeling when the occasional patient changes obstetricians. It is difficult enough when a patient moves away *midway* in a pregnancy. We *feel* this loss, too. We are both protective of and obsessive about our patients. In some cases the attachment may not be as *personal* as in others, but it is still there. Not every woman loves her obstetrician, but imagine the abandonment you would feel if, several weeks before your delivery, the doctor suddenly announced to you that he no longer *wanted* to see you. It would be difficult enough if your obstetrician were physically incapacitated and *couldn't* see you — but if he *no longer wanted to see you.* This rejection would be insulting to say the least. The obstetrician feels this same desertion whenever a patient switches physicians for whatever reason. This is all an integral part of that special bond we call the patient-physician relationship. It is mutual.

Physicians are by nature very proud people. As you read this book, pride will continually be evidenced as an essential part of the profession. The physician's responsibility for the patient's care is accepted with great pride, and this emotion is felt by the physician as well as the patient.

After finishing the book, perhaps you will understand how a proud physician, in wholesale fashion, has "abandoned" his OB patients. And it has been done with great trepidation—as has been the case with many other physicians who have been forced into making this sacrifice out of a need for self-preservation.

Being in a field of medicine that deals primarily with pregnant women is exceedingly rewarding. Can you imagine sharing the thrill of delivery on a daily basis? Some people *never* have the pleasure of sharing that much joy, especially repeatedly. Let there be no doubt that this kind of "high" exists. Ask any father who is in attendance in the delivery room for the birth of his child. The birth process is nothing short of miraculous. It is a unique mixture of awe-inspiring ecstasy mixed with deep, humbling gratitude. Can two cells (a *sperm* and an *egg*) actually become something as complex and beautiful as a living being? Even for the most cynical of skeptics, this has to make one appreciate miracles at the *divine* level. What "good fortune" to share that much happiness and to be an integral part of it on a daily basis! This is the joy of obstetrics. To be a part of the childbirth process so frequently might lead you to think it is not so *special* to the obstetrician—but it is. Each birth is still individually incredible.

This book is about the joy of OB—and about the agony, too. Unfortunately, the latter may well overshadow the former. I personally went through a slow transition wherein anxiety replaced joy as the predominant feature of obstetrical practice. Your role in this scenario will become increasingly more obvious as you read this book.

I must now relate to you how a doctor can choose a medical field that, by its very nature, has such terrible working hours. How could anyone elect to work in the middle of the night (when most normal people are sleeping)—and on weekends, too? There must be something unique and attractive about doing obstetrics. That is, it is the obstetrics itself that attracts people to this specialty. If surgery were the principal attraction, then general surgery would be the choice. If general medical care were one's primary interest, then family practice would be the choice. The same rationale holds for pediatrics, internal medicine, etc. It is obstetrics that distinguishes OB-Gyn from other specialties. It certainly is not the most lucrative field in medicine; the economics of delivering babies is not particularly rewarding when compared with the monetary remuneration in some other specialties. When office overhead and insurance premiums are considered, the fee charged by obstetricians is actually rather miserly when calculated on an hourly basis. There must be something intriguing and distinctly enjoyable about anything you elect to do—especially if it is done in the middle of the night. There are very few acts that qualify as being that exciting.

Admittedly, most obstetricians are sentimentalists. I don't say that disparagingly, but rather as a matter of fact. On repeated occasions, a warm smile from an appreciative patient is more than enough gratification, even though it may be 4:00 A.M.! Her mental uplift at your mere presence at the bedside is reward enough for having been awakened from a sound sleep or leaving a waiting room full of patients at the office. Something as simple as an apology for waking you elicits considerable personal pride in having risen to meet the challenge. You feel good in having met your commitment. A simple touch of the hand often transforms even the doctor's emotion from a feeling of inconvenience to one of joy.

There is an analogy for this with which parents can easily identify: their small child's appreciative smile at the parent's mere appearance in a time of crisis or stress. Even something mudane like a child's trip to the dentist, the pediatrician, etc., is a good example—the parent's sympathetic knowing smile is all so comforting! It is similar to a mother's smile when her lost infant *rediscovers* her, after having been lost in a store for only two minutes. This same joy and gratification for being needed and coming through in a pinch are powerful stimuli. The sense of being needed is so terribly important to us all psychologically. As physicians the need for "parenting" is manifested frequently, and the fulfillment of this need is an integral part of our daily practice. It more than justifies the sacrifice. It has nothing to do with economics. Unfortunately, economics does raise its ugly head, but this will be dealt with later.

15

Obstetricians usually become very close to their patients. We spend many months with our patients during a pregnancy, and we frequently become good friends. A very warm relationship usually develops during this prenatal period, which normally involves approximately 20 office visits. The office visits are elective and usually very pleasant. The enlarging uterus is examined and measured, the fetal heartbeat is audibly checked by obstetrician and patient alike, and the entire atmosphere is one filled with joyous anticipation about the *blessed event*. Do not think for one instant that we physicians do not feel attached to the patient, too. It is a privilege, indeed, to care for the vast majority of our ladies. Occasionally, there are exceptions; nothing is perfect. Practically and honestly speaking, though, obstetrical care is truly a fun-filled endeavor. It is a rarity for the obstetrical visit to be anything short of pleasurable for all parties involved, even the occasional mother-in-law. The patient is usually excited and happy, and the doctor identifies with the whole process. She is healthy and feels good about the situation, and the obstetrician takes great pleasure in "directing" this whole production. He gets credit for this, and rightfully so, if he practices good *preventive* medicine and minimizes complications. It is an ego trip for the doctor to officiate such happiness, and it is a gratifying experience to orchestrate such a happy symphony. It is only one's overcrowded schedule that causes office visits to be brief. Obstetricians are tender people; a feeling of attachment to their patient develops. This "love" parallels that of the patient—it is a mutual-admiration society.

This may explain the physicians's dismay and devastation when things occasionally go awry. It is an incredibly crushing blow when a newborn is anything short of perfect. The true agony of any misfortune is shared by us all. The physician's distress and sorrow will be dealt with in more detail later, but suffice it to say that the physician's joy shared in normal deliveries is more than equaled by the burden of grief when the outcome is anything less than desired.

Not only is a delivery a thrilling and exciting experience for a parent, it is just as rewarding to *do* something so *dynamic*. Lifesaving decisions can be incredibly gratifying and emotionally rewarding. After all, the ambition to be a hero or heroine was a strong, driving force behind becoming a doctor. To give aid adroitly in the occasionally difficult delivery is an extremely gratifying deed. The use of *indicated* forceps at delivery ("spoons" or "tongs" as Bill Cosby cleverly referred to them) is both challenging and gratifying when the procedure is properly performed. To perform an immediate "emergency" delivery and prevent any untoward effect upon the infant is a frightening but exciting exercise. You talk about *needing* to be needed! To perform an immediate Caesarean birth in a case of bona fide fetal distress (and literally to prevent fetal brain damage) is a most rewarding experience. Sometimes you feel like the "bionic" doctor himself! Another "high." John Denver affectionately stated it perfectly: "Far out!" It is analogous to that one booming, straight tee shot in an otherwise average round of golf: it keeps you coming back.

The miracle of conception and subsequent birth deserves reiteration. Conception itself is rather incredible: the spatial relationship between a sperm and its trip to the Fallopian tube for union with the egg is truly remarkable. It is somewhat equivalent to a person swimming from Florida to New York, against the current, and doing it in 15 minutes! The events between this first monumental task (fertilization), embryonic life, and then delivery nine months later are nothing short of miraculous. Dayenu! (This is a Jewish word whose meaning is something akin to saying: "As if that were not enough by itself!") And then the actual birth process with all of its complexities—which include the fetus's descent into the birth canal, rotating through it, flexing, then extending the head, etc. (all occurring concurrently)—is hard to imagine. The "twisting and turning" that routinely occurs is geometrically inconceivable. Then a heretofore totally aquatic creature changes its entire life support system (in only a matter of seconds!) and begins its own independent existence adapting to breathing and eating as we know them. Astonishing! Dayenu! This first breath is as awe inspiring to see as it is frightening not to see. This incredibly short trip of only inches is by far the most important journey of a lifetime. It is short, and it best be *sweet!* It is rather accurate, although trite, to say that the birth process is simply "a matter of inches." Such a statement definitely lacks the proper contrition. The birth process makes "believers" of us all.

This sequence from conception to delivery is very provocative, and it is undoubtedly a stimulus attracting many physicians to obstetrics. Still, there are many other interesting fields in this marvelous practice of skills we call medicine. The dilemma of choosing a discipline in medicine is a pleasant one; many branches of medical practice are equally gratifying. Additionally, there are certainly many fields more lucrative and less demanding of one's time—much less requiring their work to be performed "after hours." Our focus, however, will be on one group only—the endangered species: obstetricians.

I must first recount my enjoyable years in obstetrics, from the beginning in medical school through the early years in private practice. In fact, my liking for obstetrics even antedated going to medical school. My father practiced obstetrics for almost 40 years. He was an extremely well-trained surgeon "in his day," and his additional post graduate medical training in Germany in 1931 provided him the opportunity to train with several world-renowned pelvic surgeons. Because of his additional surgical training, it is not surprising that his interest in women's health care soon included first gynecology and, not long thereafter, obstetrics. I can remember my mother saying that the obstetrics was certainly a very happy part of his medical practice. "There is 'joy' in obstetrics," she would say.

In spite of my father's conspicuous absence from home, there was something unique and intriguing to me about his vocation. His sense of personal gratification from his work impressed me. His patients' admiration and gratitude instilled in me, his son, a peculiar pride and respect for him. The "M.D." after his name took on new meaning. To me that proudly meant *"my daddy"!* I would like to think that I am fortunate enough to have my title engender a similar connotation for my children.

I can remember vividly the charity delivery I witnessed as an early teenager. That very miracle of life became my inspiration. I took great delight in my new identity: "Like Poppa, like son!"

Since I entered college before my seventeenth birthday, undergraduate school was in large part a maturation process for me. A master's degree in endocrinology (the study of glands) preceded medical school and served to further my interest in women's health care. As most physicians will readily admit, the first two years of medical school were less than *ideal!* Each professor in the basic sciences (anatomy, biochemistry, physiology, etc.) had his own little *niche,* and he expected you to learn about it—in its entirety. The poor, fledgling medical student is overwhelmed with minutia. It was literally a case of not being able to see the forest for the trees. I shall never forget having to stop and literally *figure* out exactly where in the abdomen the spleen was located, yet I could draw it perfectly, identify all of its functions, nerves, blood supply, etc. I felt extremely inadequate in spite of all the little details I knew. The structures of vitamins, chemical formulae, and other *esoterica* hardly seemed pertinent to becoming a BIG DOCTOR when I would be dramatically saving lives. This is mentioned not to disparage the basic sciences, but rather to express my sentiments after having completed two years of medical school: bewildered, frustrated, eager—and all accompanied by a definite lack of glory. Repetitive acts of memorizing followed by regurgitation of the facts leaves one longing for actual patient care.

Finally, the clinical years began. And fortunately for me, I began my clinical rotation on obstetrics and gynecology. I was extremely disenchanted with medicine at this juncture, but I did have a vested interest in it by this time. Abandoning medicine and becoming a Ph.D. to do research in endocrinology had much more appeal to me at this point than did medical school. That would have meant no patient care whatsoever, and I needed to be needed! I needed to have patients.

As I began that third year of medical school, I had the pleasure of working with a resident (a doctor in specialty training in OB/Gyn) who was extremely kind and understanding of both patients *and* medical students. He was an excellent teacher and was selected the "outstanding resident" several years in a row. He was very knowledgeable and adept at teaching—plus he had the patience of Job. He could stand by calmly as it took what must have been an eternity for me to deliver a baby. He would kindly instruct me in each step, and when you worked with him, everything always seemed perfect. He was so suave, we nicknamed him "golden tongue." He always said and did the appropriate thing, and I owe him a great debt of gratitude because he was the ideal role model: a knowledgeable guy who truly loved his work. The obstetrical rotation could not have been better. We really looked forward to staying up all night and delivering babies! And to being a "real" doctor.

The rotation on OB-Gyn revealed all of the glory of obstetrics to me. The gynecology was another story! As anyone who has ever assisted on a vaginal hysterectomy can readily attest, it is a confusing operation to say the least. There is a narrow orifice through which the surgeon operates, and to the uninitiated, there are simply clamps and "strings" (sutures) attached to any number of structures. Only the surgeon can actually witness the entire operation because the operative field is so narrow. The entire operation is performed in a space that is equivalent to that of a small can of soup. I thought that the surgeon whom I was assisting was only halfway through the procedure at its conclusion! I was not sure that the patient (and probably not the vagina) was better off before or after surgery! It is almost irony that I enjoy surgery so much today after such a confusing initiation. What a difference a little knowledge makes! But back to obstetrics.

Delivering a baby is a terrific ego trip. In the absence of the fear that something might be abnormal, a delivery has to be the most rewarding, exhilerating, fun thing that OB-Gyns can do. It stirs a sense of accomplishment similar to saving someone's life, but admittedly on a lesser scale. You have the privilege of *delivering* this child to its excited parents. Even today, after literally thousands of deliveries, it is still a "fun" event. The vicarious joy you share is a fantastic feeling. I can honestly say that I have never ceased to have a warm feeling at delivery—even when the patient is totally unknown to me. Obviously, the closer you are to these patients, the greater this shared exhileration. I frequently feel my eyes well up with joy at seeing the elation parents exhibit at this event. The frequent hug I receive after the delivery of a long-standing patient is a powerfully warm exchange that is always very enlightening to me. It may be simply touching the patient or the handshake with the father, but this exchange never ceases to arouse pride and goodwill. Unfortunately, I think this elation is becoming in large part a sigh of relief! Everything is *supposed* to be perfect, and it is expected. You see, if all goes well, as explained earlier, you "tie." This problem of *expectation* is dealt with in detail in the next chapter, on consumerism. Thank goodness for ties! I have always prayed, "Dear God, I do not have to be great or famous or do wonderful things . . . just *please* do not let me 'botch' anything! Let me 'tie.' "

Even as a medical student, obstetrics was great fun for me. After all, it was as if I were a *real* doctor, indeed. It gave me a feeling of being almost divine. After all, just how omnipotent can a *mortal* be? Even such procedures as doing a circumcision were surgically challenging. The adage "to cut (properly) is to cure" became a reality. The OB-Gyn rotation was unique in that it probably allowed the student to do more things than any other third-year-medical-school rotation. It was very surprising to me that everyone did not want to go into OB at the end of our junior year of medical school. It was absolutely the most fun I could have without laughing.

Medical school took on a new complexion at this point. I now had that *needed* enthusiasm I had lacked in the basic-science years. It was perhaps equally significant that I began dating my future wife (also a medical student) at this juncture in life, so my world was now socially and academically complete.

Even though the junior medical student is at the very bottom of the "pecking order," it was a terrific feeling to be (almost) a doctor. It was so exciting to hear the word "Doctor" before your name. It was very tempting to call the hospital operator and "page" myself just to hear my name, "Doctor Freedman," over the intercom system. I enjoyed this status very much. I am still very proud of this training.

All was not rosy, however. The junior medical student is considered the very least knowledgeable person on the health care team. The nurses certainly knew more in their own little area than the student, and the "scut work" of cleaning dressings, drawing blood, and oftentimes analyzing these samples, as well as rounding up various laboratory reports, was the job delegated to the junior medical student, or JMS. The JMS is hardly considered an animal of great esteem! Even though those chores seemed menial, it was good experience, and it was instrumental in helping the JMS to become a competent physician. All of this extensive training was toward one goal: preparing the medical student to take care of the patient.

Internship ushered in the beginning of ecstasy: I got married, and I began delivering lots of babies. I was so enamored of this new found joy, I actually volunteered to take extra "night call" on occasion. Of course, I did volunteer only those nights my wife was already on call. This thrill over delivering babies continued into residency training. There was the added thrill of accomplishment in learning to perform operations expertly that heretofore had been frightening procedures. Being responsible for obstetrical patients and their delivery, as well as actually operating on *live* people, was awesome! My goodness, to think that this may actually be a lucrative endeavor someday.

Two years of military service in the army only served to foster this ego and pleasure. I literally practiced medicine, except that I was an employee of the U.S. government. It was very much akin to private practice, though. I had my *own* patients, and people at Fort Gordon actually requested that I deliver their babies. I shared this special joy of birth with many happy parents. Each time I delivered an infant, a unique emotion was aroused within me. It instilled deep humility in my heart. There was—and still is—something absolutely incredible about birth. As stated earlier, the birth process is a culmination of so many supernatural, incredible events that it is divinely electrifying.

The practice of the "art" of medicine at this point in my career was especially rewarding. I could enjoy those things that would remain so very thrilling to me even today: deliveries and surgery, coupled with the joys of an office practice. For the most part, this "practice" was with very nice people who became not only patients but friends. This unique relationship with patients truly epitomizes medicine. No other vocation enjoys such a rewarding relationship between people.

I was personally responsible for patients' care, and the onus was on my shoulders. It was a responsibility that I welcomed at that point. One never thought about being sued in those days. After all, lawsuits were only for egregious errors committed by terribly *incompetent* physicians. No well-trained "doc" ever thought about actually being sued. My naïveté in these matters typified the thinking of the average physician in the early 1970s.

Still, obstetrical practice in the army was a delightful experience because there was an excellent group of physicians, nurses, and paramedical personnel working together and enjoying medicine. It could

22

hardly be considered work. The medical care was good, our patients were very enjoyable, and the stint in the army was a pleasant experience.

For the first time, it was not just therapeutic medicine (treating sick people)—disease prevention and wellness care were included. I have the strong personal conviction that good health is a divine blessing—the only gratitude He requires is its maintenance. Stressing the important benefits of hormone therapy such as oral contraceptives and estrogen replacement therapy in the menopause is a good example. Educating patients about the many benefits and allaying anxiety about the risks continue to be a challenge even today because only 10 to 12 percent of healthy women take advantage of such hormone therapy. It is always rewarding to physicians to provide medications and therapies that will improve patients' life-style and quality of life. This is all part of "being needed."

The next step in this enjoyable practice was my going into private practice and being granted a part-time faculty appointment at the Medical College of Georgia. This afforded me the best of both worlds, academic medicine and the chance to have an enjoyable private practice. No one could design a better opportunity: your very own private patients, an opportunity to teach medical students and residents on OB-Gyn, and at the same time make a very comfortable living.

This seemed too good to be true. And it was. There is no denying that a physician does see some patients who are unpleasant and/or overbearing. There are always some people who can absolutely ruin any day. But then again, I know that I do not fulfill each and every patient's needs. Furthermore, I am realistic enough to know that there are surely some patients who have been disappointed in the care they received. This may not have been by design, but it is unfortunately a reality. All things being equal though, well over 95 percent of one's private patients *are* fun to see and treat. I am not being overly dramatic in stating that it is honestly a privilege to provide them their care. What a pleasure to be needed, and it is equally gratifying to provide satisfaction.

A problem exists because a certain percentage of patients will be less than pleased with their care—for whatever reason. Part of this dissatisfaction may be because of unrealistic expectations. Yet some patients' dissatisfaction may be the result of truly substandard medical care. If this is the case, then by all means, let us as physicians help rectify the situation. Perhaps more importantly, let us prevent its recurrence! The rest of this book attempts to define the problem of medical malpractice as it exists today (primarily in obstetrics but also in medicine in general) and to offer some solution to the present crisis—yes, CRISIS. As you will see, your participation is desperately needed and mandatory if we are to improve and preserve the best medical care system in the world.

The early years were truly a delightful experience. In writing this book, I am repeatedly amazed at the emotions generated when I reflect upon the transition from happiness to misery which occurred over a 10- to 15-year period. Pleasure has been replaced by a sense of uneasiness. There is the constant threat of legal action should the outcome of childbirth not be a perfect one. This anxiety becomes unbearable and inescapable. The reason apprehension is so dominant is that practicing good medicine and providing quality care for patients will not protect you from being sued. This constant threat of suit gives no respite.

I have had the sad chore of explaining to many patients that, regrettably, I would be unable to deliver their baby. Almost without exception, this has generated some feelings of genuine anger on *my* part. Perhaps hostility would be a better term. At any rate, each explanation to a patient elicits a very strong emotion on my part. A "loving" relationship with patients is being transformed into an adversarial one because of the litigious climate. This change in the patient-physician relationship is terribly disturbing to physicians, and we are justifiably angry about it. We enjoy "liking" our patients; enjoy our obligation to patients; and this is especially true in obstetrics. Being forced to view patients as potential adversaries is terribly unpleasant and disconcerting to doctors.

My patients have been exceedingly understanding. Patients' genuine empathy has only served to enhance my feelings of remorse. The real constant in this setting has been my hostility—hostility because I was lured into obstetrics because of all the many pleasantries associated with treating young, happy, healthy ladies. These pleasantries have fallen prey to many unjust modifications. This unrelenting attack is beginning to take its toll. A real exodus from the specialty is under way.

CHAPTER 3

Consumerism: Patients' Expectations

MEDICINE IS constantly changing, and fortunately this is usually in the form of progress. As with any form of change, medicine included, the risk/benefit ratio must be kept in mind. It would be rather utopian and naïve to think that some compromise is not necessary in achieving progress. We, as health-care professionals, must remain adaptable, but, at the same time, we must remember that consumerism may initiate change that occasionally has no scientific basis (or benefit). In this context, consumerism may be defined as how the consumer (in this case, the patient) influences how the provider (the physician) practices medicine. In fact, this influence may even be counterproductive and, in some instances, detrimental to optimum health care.

There is no denying the fact that progress has been made in reducing complications in obstetrics. This applies to both the mother and the newborn alike. Pediatricians and obstetricians have worked very diligently in reducing the risks for both patients involved in the childbirth process. Prematurity remains the leading cause of mortality in newborns, and our pediatric colleagues are responsible for truly laudable improvements in the care and survival of these high-risk infants. These advances have been relatively unencumbered by consumerism in pediatrics.

Medicine—that is, pediatrics—can be practiced as an art and a science without a great deal of outside interference. The delivery of markedly premature babies in hospitals staffed with neonatalogists and properly equipped nurseries has been a major factor in improving the survival of these premature babies, affectionately referred to as "premies." Transfer of the mother before delivery, or of the "premie" shortly after delivery, oftentimes is met with minor consumer disdain, but the unquestioned benefits of transfers to sophisticated medical

27

centers justifies any inconvenience encountered by the patient. There are occasional instances when the patient must accept the physician's judgment. Oftentimes this decision may not please us either, but if it is deemed necessary, it has to be done.

Compared with pediatrics, however, obstetrics is not quite so fortunate and frequently is more subject to consumerism. Consumerism in this instance refers primarily to the expectations of all patients to have a normal, simple delivery of a healthy baby. This becomes somewhat of a paradox. Because medicine has made such great strides in recent years, patients have almost come to expect minor miracles as the order of the day. In previous generations, a markedly premature birth was accompanied by demise at or shortly after birth. With the advent of advanced neonatal care, many of these extremely premature infants now survive. Unfortunately, some of these survivors may exhibit some residual effect as a result of their premature birth. This impaired infant frequently presents hardships, financial burdens, and other inconveniences which may understandably lead to some hostility, anger, and/or disappointment by the family involved. Given such an outcome, it is only natural to scrutinize the events associated with labor and delivery very closely. If unrealistic goals have been previously engendered via overzealous consumerism, the outcome becomes even more difficult to accept, and anger is sometimes aroused. This one emotion—anger—is probably the one constant in all medical-legal action.

This chapter will address the issue of consumerism as it relates specifically to obstetrics. It reviews some of the changes consumerism has initiated—both good and bad—whereas the malpractrice issue per se is dealt with in great detail in later chapters. These two issues, consumerism and malpractice, are somewhat inseparable, however. A recent quote from Elvoy Raines is rather exemplary: "The astonishing increase in the frequency and severity of medical malpractice litigation is directly attributable to rising consumerism."[1]* Our discussion

---

*Elvoy Raines is a noted authority on obstetrical medical malpractice professional liability. He was Associate Director, Government Relations, the American College of OB-Gyn, in 1985.

here, however, will be directed principally toward consumerism rather than malpractice.

As consumers, patients are naturally in search of good, quality service. They usually accomplish this goal with cost containment in mind. Additionally, comparability to services received by friends and/ or relatives is often sought. This is well and good, but, at the same time, certain expectations are generated. In terms of modern obstetrics, these expectations are great expectations regarding perfect outcomes. These preconceived ideas are a logical sequence of events. All mothers should enjoy labor, and all infants should be healthy. No one would argue with this, but these expectations cannot always be met. As physicians, and perhaps especially so as obstetricians, we have contributed unintentionally to what at times may be great but unattainable expectations.

In addition to creating great expectations and unattainable goals, some physicians occasionally allow changes to be instituted as a result of the pressure of such consumerism; therefore, these changes may not be the result of scientific knowledge or fact. Such change without proven merit cannot be considered "progress." Several examples of this behavior may prove illustrative.

The occasional conflict of interest between consumer and the medical establishment may at times be only a reflection of a difference in social attitudes (that is, a challenge of authority). As progressives, physicians should be attuned to their patients' desires and pleasures. I can remember very well the president of the American College of Obstetrics and Gynecology making a policy statement some 20 years ago regarding the presence of expectant fathers in the delivery room. He said, "I always give the father a choice concerning being present in the delivery room: him or me!" This was the attitude of the "establishment" some 20 years ago, and it was a hotly debated issue at that time. There were equal numbers of obstetricians pro and con. This type of change (husbands present at delivery) has been a wholesome and healthy change, even though it may have been contrary to the accepted policy at that time. Such a change was good, and it certainly did no harm.

Not everything new can be condoned simply to allow the patient to

29

"do her own thing." As obstetricians, we have an obligation to ensure that such changes are indeed without hazard. Besides, when anything does work to the detriment of the patient, (or her infant), who do you imagine will be directly responsible? The physician, of course! An example of this occurred recently in our hospital wherein a patient and her husband insisted on keeping their infant with them in the birthing room for a protracted period of time. This occurred in spite of repeated requests by the nursing staff to take the infant to the nursery. The couple wanted an exceedingly prolonged time with the infant to promote "bonding," although it was clearly the father who was so adamant in his request. The parents finally acquiesced and allowed the infant to be taken to the nursery after some 45 minutes in the cool environment of the birthing room. This delay in getting the infant into the nursery was the direct result of the parents' insistence, and it was in spite of considerable protest from the nursing staff. When the newborn did arrive in the nursery, its body temperature was extremely depressed, and the infant subsequently became quite ill. Fortunately, the infant recovered without incident.

The husband was irate and quite verbal about not paying the bill and "bringing suit" because the infant became ill after initially having been healthy. His contention was that the nurses should have *intervened!* and should have coerced him to transfer the infant to the nursery. This parent's action is detrimental to the system. Rebuking authority figures as a part of consumerism is totally unacceptable. In fact, it is the father who probably should be prosecuted for an indirect form of child abuse.

We as obstetricians should remind fathers or "significant others" that it is a privilege and an honor to be present in the delivery room— not an obligation. We should remind them that as obstetricians, we are glad that they are present. Yet let us make no mistake about it: their presence is intended to play a *support* role for the laboring patient. Furthermore, we as obstetricians will go to great lengths and work very hard with him in accomplishing that goal of supporting our patient. All too often though, we fail to stress the limitations and expectations of this supporting actor. It should be stated emphatically that he is an invited guest in the delivery room.

Consumerism: Patients' Expectations

The dominant "player" in this scene is the laboring lady. It is extremely frustrating to an obstetrician to be forced at times to convince a rather idealistic father-to-be that his wife is suffering from what to her at that point may be *intense* discomfort. The expectant father sometimes stands by idly, complimenting his spouse on how well she is doing, as she pleads desperately for some help. From his perspective, a completely natural childbirth is ideal. That is not the question at this point in time. From her perspective, the need for something to relieve the pain is the paramount issue. Obstetricians have sometimes been forced to justify to a labor coach the medicating of an uncomfortable laboring patient. The safety and benefit of such medication certainly support its use, but an occasional expectant father resents any form of interference and makes the obstetrician's job needlessly more difficult. This situation is occasionally made worse when a Lamaze instructor may become a little overenthusiastic in her emphasis on nonintervention and natural childbirth.

The relief or tolerance of discomfort in labor should be a very individual situation. It should be the topic of considerable discussion during the entire pregnancy, well in advance of labor. Many variables may be involved in labor and delivery, and alternative strategies can be discussed. Decisions are based on so many factors that the course of the labor and delivery must be made to be adaptable; frequently, it may change as the labor progresses. The situation is somewhat akin to a ballgame wherein the "game plan" is modified depending on how the game evolves. It is unwise to be adamant about a predetermined method of delivery, and it is essential that this plan be based on the knowledge that different situations may dictate using alternative methods. The adage "Necessity is the mother of invention" is sometimes quite appropriate in obstetrics.

The advent of childbirth classes has been a marvelous addition to the quality of patient care. It is another example of change in the form of progress. Not only is the laboring patient educated about labor and delivery, but frequently her partner or coach in childbirth is also duly prepared to be helpful. It should be reemphasized at this point that the role of the "significant other" is truly one of support to the laboring patient and not the reverse. The patient is the dominant figure. This point requires constant reemphasis, especially for an occasional male chauvinist who does not recognize his role as one of support for his partner. Having such *informed* couples in labor and delivery has been a real boon to modern obstetrics. It has added to the joy of obstetrics in most instances.

The concept of childbirth education has been championed throughout the world, and it has alleviated tremendous anxiety in quite a number of patients. It has benefited literally millions of frightened prospective mothers. A potentially terrifying experience has been made into an experience to be anticipated with great pleasure. The fear of the unknown (childbirth) has been openly discussed and explained, and when such education is done properly, the knowledge gained allows the experience of labor to be not only tolerable but actually enjoyable. A valuable patient education service has been formulated, and it has been implemented almost universally. Obstetricians owe a debt of gratitude to many enthusiastic childbirth educators. Their efforts have not been met with great acceptance by all obstetricians, and it is only through perseverence that this tremendous service of patient education has continued to gain acceptance.

Although the education itself is of unquestionable benefit, the demands that have arisen from the preparation process may not be quite so totally desirable from a medical standpoint. Some of the ideas presented to the prospective mother are without documentation or proven benefit. On occasion, the material and views presented in the classes are primarily those of the individual instructor, and the education is then based not on fact but on his or her experience as a childbirth educator. Fortunately, these views are usually taught with *sound* obstetrics as the very foundation of the whole process, and rightfully so, but not always. Classes on preparing for childbirth must stress good medical care as their principal prerequisite. In no way should these classes generate such overly enthusiastic expectations that good medicine might be compromised in attempting to satisfy them. For instance, to suggest not having intravenous (IV) fluids during active labor so as to allow the patient freedom of movement during labor may serve as a good illustration. The vast majority of obstetricians firmly believes that an IV is necessary at the time of delivery for the possible emergency administration of medication, etc. This is in no way a conspiracy by physicians to be obstructive to patients—it is simply a precautionary procedure that is hoped is only minimally inconvenient to the patient. There may be times when the obstetrician may feel an IV is not necessary, but this must be at the physician's discretion, based on the medical circumstances—not the patient's convenience. For the obstetrician to be forced to justify the use of IV fluids during labor is somewhat perturbing and even annoying at times.

Let me elaborate. Childbirth classes frequently involve numerous couples. A subtle inference about eliminating a "restrictive IV" necessitates considerable countercounseling by the physician. This becomes very time consuming on a one-on-one basis in the doctor's office. The obstetrician may have to discuss the subject with each individual patient who has heard such an idealistic promotion in a childbirth class. Again, this is a discussion which is totally the result of overzealous educators expressing their opinions about seeking less interference in the birthing process, that is, a more "natural" childbirth. Eliminating a "restrictive" IV at delivery in no way enhances good medical care, but rather may be deleterious. It simply bespeaks consumerism.

The childbirth educator sometimes assumes the role of a self-appointed authority figure. This may not be by his or her own design or desire, but it does sometimes happen. My allegation that the childbirth educator may sometimes assume such a role might be offensive to some para-professional who teaches childbirth classes. It is not my purpose to insult anyone, but rather to illustrate a point. In other words, childbrith preparation and education should be exactly that: *preparation* and *education* for the delivery and the labor process. It is not a course to educate the pregnant patient in what good medical care is or should include. Good medical care is solely the responsibility of the physician. Good medical care requires knowledge learned by the physician through extensive medical education over a long period of time. The quality of the medical care as such should not be the focus of the childbirth class. The patient's preparation for delivery is the focus of these classes. Let us prepare our patients for the pregnancy and the delivery, and let us do this through childbirth educators. At the same time, let us remember also that patients cannot be taught everything that good obstetrical care entails simply by attending several classes, nor should this be attempted. These instructors are educators in preparing for childbirth—not educators in assessing the quality of medical care. If the childbirth educator has some problem with the medical care itself, then this should be discussed with the physician and not presented as a personal vendetta in a prenatal class. The physician is ultimately the responsible party, and as the most knowledgeable member of the health care team, the doctor must be certain that patients are properly prepared and informed.

All too often, our own bias, and sometimes personal knowledge, can interfere with the process of educating others. It is very helpful to set specific goals and then structure the learning process to attain them. In this view, anything we can teach expectant parents that is *helpful* during childbirth is a real service to them, but we must keep our goals clearly in mind.

Let us turn our attention now to childbirth education and the expectations it can create. This is very closely related to consumerism. Many para-professionals—physicians' assistants, nurses, Lamaze instructors, etc.—can be educators. Physicians are educators, too. We all are capable of generating tremendous enthusiasm. This enthusiasm may create an anticipation of unrealistic goals unattainable by even the best of medical care. This is especially true if popularity and consumerism are at stake. Sometimes, circumstances in labor and delivery dictate that almost all of a patient's expectations must be altered. There may be heavy disappointment. The patient may even, at times, feel robbed. Quality medical care must still prevail, however, even at the cost of popularity. Rare is the obstetrician who has been spared playing the role of "spoiler" at one time or another. The situation is made infinitely more difficult when childbirth has been so emphasized and made to be such an essential part of motherhood.

I have great empathy for the disappointed patient who, because of medical complications, has been forced to miss this "natural" experience. I think experiencing natural childbrith has become an expectation, almost a necessity, that health care providers created, and at times perhaps even overemphasized. It may well be more perception than reality. The question could certainly be debated, I admit, but suffice it to say a mother may feel somewhat "flat" and "empty" when this "pleasure" which has been so strongly anticipated is denied her because of complications beyond anyone's control. Great anticipation may then become great disappointment, and occcasionally this scenario generates some hostility or anger. As previously mentioned, anger is a common denominator in the medical jurisprudence problem. It is truly an essential ingredient.

As sensitive people, obstetricians usually recognize this perceived "loss." A "guilt trip" by the occasional disappointed patient or husband is the very last thing the physician needs when he may be scrambling around making preparations for an emergency Caesarean section. This is usually not an obstacle as such in obstetrical care, but the example does serve to illustrate how consumerism can make the practice of obstetrics a little more complex and difficult. Fortunately, most patients have been helpful in emergencies even though they may be terribly disappointed and oftentimes very frightened.

It is partly because of this education and childbirth preparation that the experience of labor and delivery becomes one of such great anticipation. This is by design and this is good; yet how, in this process of education, did we fail to explain to the patient that her obstetrician is very well aware of her emotions and her sense of anticipation? In fact, we obstetricians share her goals even though we must on occasion deny her of this pleasure. We are very anxious for her to enjoy natural childbirth, but not at the expense of good medicine. After all, it is good medical care that remains our primary responsibility. It is not *education* that serves as a source of consternation for the physician, but rather the *failure* to educate the expectant mother of possible complications that sometimes cause grief when great expectations are not realized. To reemphasize my point, then, the principal of quality medical care must take precedence over personal desires and should remain unencumbered by consumerism. If personal desires are met, terrific —but the standard of care *must* be met.

It would be a grave injustice to portray labor and delivery as anything less than a "critical care" area. Although labor and delivery *may* be a fun-filled experience in the majority of cases, complications can

35

arise. We cannot afford to be lulled into a false sense of security by the infrequency of serious complications. For the most part, we can and should expect to enjoy labor and delivery—but not at the expense of being unprepared for those instances when unpopular decisions are necessary.

Other reservations with regard to consumerism are noteworthy. An episiotomy, the small incision made at the time of delivery, is a good example. Obstetricians do not perform episiotomies because of any innate desire to do any extra sewing. This incision is necessary (when it is done) to prevent a tear of the tissue between the vagina and the rectum. Where does any medical evidence suggest that *necessary* surgery should be avoided? Surgical incisions heal very neatly and very well from side to side, so the actual length of an incision is not even a primary feature. A "tear" in tissue, however, oftentimes results in irregular edges, abrasions, and devitalized tissue. In spite of this fact, patients frequently request their obstetricians to avoid an episiotomy. I present this request to avoid episiotomy as an example of meddlesome consumerism. Natural birth without episiotomy is the goal of activist groups who feel that obstetricians are caught up more in tradition than in good patient care. I can assure you, nothing could be further from the truth. Good obstetricians are delighted to avoid an episiotomy whenever it is deemed unnecessary. It is only reasonable to expect childbirth preparation classes to include discussion of the possibilities of such "necessary surgery" rather than to disparage or discourage the practice critically.

It is worth reemphasizing that change per se is not inherently bad. We must, however, constantly assess whether the new idea or method is superior to the one in existence. More importantly, we must be absolutely sure that it is in no way harmful. There should be some scientific study and rationale behind change. Many current methods or modifications of delivery, even though they may be popular, may not prove to be beneficial in any way for either the mother or the infant. There is very little scientific documentation that such things as a Leboyer delivery (dim lights, immersing the newborn in a warm water bath, etc.) is in any way superior to conventional deliveries. Some procedures may even be dangerous in some respects. Again, documentation is necessary to substantiate such a change. It requires more than just enthusiasm to warrant support for new ideas. No physician is opposed to change that will improve either the mother's or the infant's health. After all, improved care is a universal goal of physicians and patients alike. No one is adverse to alternative systems that prove to be beneficial. Taken one step further, we try to accommodate patients whenever possible. Unfortunately, on occasion, every obstetrician experiences the rare situation in which the more he or she acquiesces and allows, the more ridiculous the patient's requests become. I recently had a patient who made so many foolish, yet innocuous, requests that I felt personally obligated to deliver her; yes, *obligated*. I was too embarrassed to have one of my partners deliver such a demanding patient. She and her husband were terribly persistent (insistent might be more accurate) in their demands. They were also rather critical of everything—my office, the nurses, the receptionists, etc., *ad infinitum*. I have more respect for my partners than to have allowed one of them to endure this abuse at delivery, so I felt I had an obligation to avoid their coming into contact with this couple. Such patients invite contempt from all with whom they come in contact. My mistake in this case was in not suggesting early in her pregnancy that the patient change obstetricians. Once I became uncomfortable with her irrational requests, I should have attempted to terminate her care or instructed her at least to try to accept what we expected in our practice. I have terminated patients' care only twice in my entire practice, but it was certainly a relief in both cases. One patient wanted to know why I didn't use a sterile speculum to do her PAP smear. I told her that the vagina was not a sterile cavity. She wanted to know why the technician did her blood pressure and not I, and why was I not present at her sonogram. She questioned *everything*. It was a relief finally to say, "I do not wish to answer any more of your outrageous questions." I felt relieved when I told her, "You make practicing medicine terribly unpleasant for me!" Just as the patient may choose, the physician would do well to remember that he or she too may have a choice in the matter.

When the patient-physician relationship becomes strained, it is time to suggest a change. As adults, we must all realize that occasionally conflicts in personality will occur, and when this happens, we must both be mature enough to recognize it, admit it, and make the necessary change. In such cases, it may be far better to suggest to the patient that she change obstetricians than to risk animosity in the patient-physician relationship.

Another recent, personal experience in reference to consumerism is worthy of mention. A patient had requested not to be monitored in labor—that is, she had pleaded not to have a continuous fetal heart-rate tracing obtained during her labor. She just felt "confined" with a monitoring device attached to her abdomen. I cajoled almost to the point of coercion, and she finally agreed to be monitored. She was the very patient who had a sudden and unheralded placental separation necessitating an immediate emergency Caesarean section. There was absolutely no time to spare and every—but every—second was preciously important. The infant had a good APGAR score (the initial evaluation at birth) and was healthy, thanks to the monitor and the immediate Caesarean section. There is no doubt in my mind that considerable, valuable time would have been lost in diagnosing this condition, recognizing the catastrophe, and expediently delivering the baby had we acquiesced to her initial request and allowed her the "freedom" of not being monitored so closely. To this very day she is *extremely* grateful—but not nearly so grateful as I!

In some ways, we as obstetricians have also fostered consumerism. We have rightfully encouraged a casual, relaxed atmosphere in labor and delivery. Comfortable, home-style surroundings are the order of the day, and television is often provided in many labor rooms, and family and friends are encouraged to visit "at will." This is fine, and it is presented as positive change. We must not forget, however, that labor and delivery is a critical-care area, and labor is not without hazard. There are many dangers inherent in the delivery process, and, as any obstetrician will readily admit, complications can arise when we least expect them. This is the principal reason most obstetricians are adverse to "birthing centers" and domiciliary delivery systems. Very unexpected and frequently life-threatening complications can and do occur, and this is the single most important reason behind having the necessary sophisticated equipment available in an accredited hospital setting. The availability of ancillary life-support systems, operating rooms, etc., is certainly an expense, but when it is necessary, there is no room for compromise in a bona fide emergency. The labor and delivery area is definitely an acute-care area.

Whenever cost containment (another feature of consumerism) is considered, an interesting analogy can be drawn between the coronary care unit and the labor and delivery (CCU versus L&D) area. The equipment is even similar in a number of ways. Each unit is a recognized acute-care area where the primary task is one of monitoring patients' vital functions on a minute-to-minute and sometimes "beat-to-beat" basis. A relaxed atmosphere is to be encouraged, but, again, this should not be at the expense of appropriate critical-care capability.

Everyone agrees that the octogenarian, the eighty-year-old, must be admitted to the hospital and monitored and observed very carefully when he is ill: "The patient could die at any minute!" This is very true, and that very fact is exactly why the patient must be monitored so very closely. This point is not in dispute. When we look at simple longevity, a startling fact arises: Even in the best of circumstances, and with the absolute *greatest* care, how much quality, productive life are we prolonging? This is not to suggest that we alter our approach to the aged; this is not to suggest to anyone that we should not "go for it." It is simply intended to point out an enormous discrepancy: Days of life are at stake; maybe a few years. Yet for the laboring patient and her infant, we are talking decades and perhaps even generations! When one considers the fifty-odd years of longevity of the laboring mother *and* the prospective eighty-plus years of her infant, the parallel in critical-care areas between the CCU and the L&D area is no longer applicable. From an economic or a statistical perspective, we should be spending billions on the acute-care situation in labor and delivery. Because of the great potential of the laboring mother and her infant, we can ill-afford to skimp. Yes, it can be expensive. Please note, that I would in no way take anything away from coronary care units. The purpose of this analogy is to illustrate how terribly important the labor and delivery area is and that is must be properly considered an acute-care unit. To consider it otherwise is shortsighted.

Another analogy is in order. In the CCU, the nurses receive extensive training in not only cardiology but also electrocardiography. This specialized training concentrates on the heart and rightly so. The nurses spend weeks learning about heart tracings, drugs used in their patients, and the various intricacies of such a specialized unit. This training is important and is time very well spent. There is certification required upon completion of the training, and the examinations are rather comprehensive. This ensures quality control, which is so vital in any critical-care area. As in any specialty area, there are mechanisms for adjusting the nurses' salaries accordingly. This is a part of the CCU system and, again, a prerequisite to quality care. I commend them in their organization and sophistication. This system, based on merit, is admirable.

Now, let us consider labor and delivery. As will be recalled, it was stated that we have made labor and delivery a relaxed, domiciliary-type facility. That is fine. Change as a part of progress is good, but labor and delivery is still an acute-care area. The nurses in labor and delivery should be equally "specialized." Their training should include in-depth knowledge of fetal heart-rate patterns and of labor itself and should probably culminate in proper certification. It is unfair to nurses to ask them to function in such a highly specialized acute-care area without proper training. Accordingly, L&D nurses should be compensated properly for the extensive training and certification just like coronary care nurses. It is indeed a mistake not to consider the labor and delivery area a true critical-care facility. Constant surveillance of the patient is mandatory. A cavalier attitude, so often connected with childbrith, may not be entirely in our patients' best interest. A reminder that consumerism must not compromise the quality of care is in order. To sacrifice technological advances in favor of a more relaxed atmosphere can hardly be labeled "progress." This perhaps represents regression rather than progression. This is not to imply dehumanization, but simply to call attention to proper detail and an awareness of the potential hazards. It is still inconceivable for me to think that the availability of an immediate Caesarean section is not an absolute prerequisite for any delivery facility. Could a coronary care unit be approved without ready access to a defibrillator (electrical heart stimulator)?

Let us return then to consumerism and the part it plays in obstetrics. We must not be lured into complacency by the anticipated pleasant expectations and normal, simple deliveries. Ninety-five percent of obstetrics may very well be uncomplicated and seem completely routine. Obstetricians have learned to identify with this rather relaxed, enjoyable atmosphere. In some specialities this may even lead to boredom. In obstetrics, however, we must be ever aware of the potential disasters and the rapidity with which they can develop. We cannot afford to be so relaxed as to allow changes that might hinder our ability to meet any emergency. The idea of not having IV fluids present at the time of delivery is a prime example. It is perhaps an inconvenience, but, in those situations where it is truly needed, it is lifesaving. Certainly, no anesthesiologist would elect to put a patient to sleep for major surgery without having first started an IV. This is "just in case," and it is done in spite of the fact that the operation may be routine and not even life threatening. Most physicians love having this type of added "insurance." Far better to have it and not need it than the reverse. The same rationale may be applicable to critical-care areas throughout the hospital. I feel sure other areas of the hospital suffer the pressures of consumerism also. L&D simply feels these pressures more acutely.

As obstetricians, we shall continue to strive to improve the provisions of health care while, at the same time, allowing considerable freedom of choice to our patients. We must remain sensitive to our patients' requests. We must not, however, accept alternative methods of health care without proper documentation. Although being popular is nice and bolsters the ego, we should not fall victim to consumerism at the expense of proven sound medicine. Let us define progress as some measure of an improvement in our delivery of health care. Yielding to activist pressure as a part of consumerism may not be synonymous with progress in all instances. If we as obstetricians are the most knowledgeable member of the team providing care for the pregnant woman, it remains our specific responsibility to ensure that change does indeed represent progress.

Consumerism has also led to the developement of some very unrealistic goals—that is, every delivery should culminate in the delivery of a healthy, *perfect* infant, with no resultant injury to the mother. Furthermore, this should always be accomplished while being a pleasant experience for all those involved. While this is also the sincere goal of all obstetricians, it is in no way attainable. It is similar to setting a goal suggesting that there will be no complications from a surgical procedure. The only surgeon who has *no* complications is a surgeon who does very little or no surgery. No matter how good you are, you cannot "bat 1,000" all the time. No physician is perfect.

Very plainly stated, there is an accepted, unavoidable rate of complication in obstetrics. In this field of medicine, there are 2 to 3 infants per 100 live births that have abnormalities, some of which may even be fatal or severely compromising. This is a statistical norm. This is *in spite of* the very best of care. When the hoped-for typical fairy-tale ending does not happen, it is only natural that disappointment and heartache ensue. This *hurt* is also felt by the physician because he or she identifies so closely with the patient. Few emotions can be as painful as the one associated with the discovery that the fetal heartbeat has ceased and the baby is no longer alive. Each time this happens—and it happens with just enough frequency to make every obstetrician a little nervous—you, the obstetrician, lose a little of your own heartbeat. Anytime you deliver an infant with a significant anomaly (for example, a cleft lip and/or palate), you suffer the same emotional upheaval that the patient does upon the discovery of the anomaly. That same feeling of having personally lost something terribly vital to you is aroused once again. The loss is often felt as a giant hollow in the middle of your stomach, and a peculiar wave of nausea often accompanies it. These emotions are not easily forgotten. They haunt you for days— even weeks. It is a grief that stays with you 24 hours a day for any number of days. If you are an obstetrician, you must expect occasional complications and disappointments. But they always hurt. The patient feels tremendous grief and acute loss; there is no denying that. And, thank goodness, few people ever have to endure that again. But the obstetrician has the dubious distinction of living this emotion repeatedly. The more unexpected it is, the more severe the emotional upheaval. Just as there is joy in obstetrics, there is sorrow.

I remember one delivery of several years ago, and it remains as clear to me as if it were yesterday. A physician's wife had an uneventful prenatal course, labor, and a very normal, uncomplicated delivery. After one initial gasp, the infant ceased respiratory effort and literally began to die before our very eyes! In spite of resuscitory efforts for what seemed an eternity, there was no response. You can imagine how devastated all three of us were. I immediately retraced her entire pregnancy, labor, delivery, and resuscitation efforts. I admonished myself (without reason), and, as I reflected, I questioned whether I had made some horrible mistake and was guilty of some dreadful oversight. The feeling of having possibly made some grave mistake is so undeniably present, threatening, and so unpleasant, it defies description. I suppose it might be compared to discovering your child missing and the gate to your front yard open, and all you can see are speeding cars racing down the street in front of your house. "Did I leave the gate open?" It is simply a "sick" feeling because of the sense of incrimination involved. It may be unfounded, but it is still present. Being absolved of guilt offers little solace. Finding the child safe is the only true relief, and until you do that, the pain and suffering are insurmountable. Exoneration in this situation did come at autopsy with the discovery of extremely underdeveloped and nonfunctional lungs. The infant's lungs simply had not developed properly. The initial pain and grief that the family and I experienced are vivid even today. But it was at least made bearable, since I was able to find out from the autopsy that I was in no way *responsible* for the occurrence. This stressful emotion has nothing to do with malpractice. It is simply a genuine grief reaction shared with the family. My purpose in mentioning this particular incident here is to reiterate how we as obstetricians have done ourselves somewhat of a disservice in regard to overemphasizing the relaxed atmosphere and building such great expectations without reminding our patients of the potential risks and complications. It is not that we should instill any undue fear or anxiety in our patients, but inherent in generating such great enthusiasm should be a patient-doctor contract alluding to the understanding that problems can and do occur. The great expectations must be accompanied by the realization that it is not a perfect world, and it is not always possible to have the fairy-tale ending. Physicians are mortal, and we will always do our very best, but we cannot be held responsible for all things—accountable for all things, yes, but not responsible. Let us as obstetricians welcome this accountability. The controversy over responsibility versus accountability is one of the real factors—contentions—among those of us who are "bailing out" of obstetrics. We accept *accountability* but not *responsibility* for an imperfect child, no matter what. Too often, good medicine has been practiced, but the responsibility for a poor outcome has been charged to the physician. This is unacceptable to proud, sincere health care providers. If you give a concerted 100-percent effort to a cause, that is obviously the limit of what you can offer.

Mortals can do no more. Nor should any more be expected. To "tie" (i.e., to have a normal outcome from a delivery) is a welcome relief. The good outcome is now expected; it becomes the "norm." Anything less than perfect becomes totally unacceptable (i.e., a "loss"). If quality health care is not sufficient to exonerate the physician, then he or she becomes defenseless. Such vulnerability leads to an incessant anxiety that can become intolerable. And it has already—to far too many obstetricians!

NOTES

1. Roberts, D. K., Shane, J. A., Roberts, M. L., eds. Confronting the malpractice crisis: guidelines for the obstetrician-gynecologist. Kansas City: Eagle Press, 1985; 115.

CHAPTER 4

What Malpractice Means
to the Physician

MEDICAL SCHOOL is a rather grueling experience. Not only is there a considerable time commitment, but the whole endeavor is terribly stressful. Because competition for the opportunity to pursue this career is so keen, I felt fortunate even to be there, yet not so grateful to be so persecuted. None the less, it is an "honor" that the medical student appreciates and accepts with considerable pride. Graduation confers that heralded title: Doctor of Medicine. With that title go a certain dignity, a sense of accomplishment, and a suggestion of respect. Graduation represents a major milestone. You are now a "doctor," and no one can take that title away from you. Graduation, and more specifically having received a degree, relieves a certain amount of pressure and anxiety. A goal has been reached; you have successfully met the requirement. Inherent in that title, however, is an enormous commitment. Immediately after graduation one feels a sense of honor—and a tremendous responsibility. In fact, the delusions of grandeur are brief, soon to be replaced by the reality of being a practicing physician. Simply stated, people's very lives will depend upon your competence. No one enters an internship after graduation without considerable trepidation. "Will I perform up to the expected standard?"

One theme is constant throughout medical training: honor and integrity. This continues regardless of what specialty training one chooses. Physicians are always aware of becoming more proficient at the primary objective, healing the sick, but many subthemes exist. Whether healing the sick involves relieving pain, literally cutting out disease, or practicing preventive medicine, the goal is always the same: Do it well and to the very best of your ability. Why? Not because fees depend upon it, but because of the intense personal dedication to the profession and the honor that goes along with simply being a physician. Personal pride, integrity, and that feeling of dedication are simply a way of life. There is no statute that requires it, but it is the unwritten law, and it is deeply ingrained by the time one's training is complete.

Those specific qualities—integrity and honor—make medicine a uniquely distinct profession. It is different from all other forms of vocation—except perhaps the ministry. Honor and dignity reign supreme. Only the ministry is afforded so much trust and total confidentiality. There are certainly times when the physician does not know all of the answers in medical dilemmas; this is not to be denied and should never be a source of dismay. Shame on any physician who is too proud to say he or she does not know something! It can be expected, and should be readily admitted, that the occasional diagnosis (or even cure) may be elusive—and this is a recognized limitation of all physicians. No one can be expected to know all of the answers, and this frailty is one which is readily admitted to patients repeatedly. This mortal imperfection is readily accepted by even the most egotistical of physicians. Regardless of the expectations, there *are* limitations.

It is perfectly acceptable to be "uncertain" at times in the practice of medicine. More laboratory work or other studies may be in order. The physician should gladly admit to being human; not knowing *something* happens to us on a daily basis. One fact remains perfectly clear throughout medical training: You do not fake it. You must be thoroughly honest. There is no punishment for not being the very first to make a diagnosis. Although there is certainly a premium on being a fantastic diagnostician and/or technician, honesty and integrity remain much more important than being the very first to recognize a condition. The *honesty* is the constant. Knowledge can be lacking, but honesty must persist indefinitely. Being "top gun" is admirable, but by definition there can be only *one*, and that distinction is surely very temporary. Medicine does not require that you be top gun. A standard of care is established, and physicians are expected to meet it. Anything less is totally unacceptable. There is universal agreement about this.

Should it then come as any great surprise that being accused of substandard practice—specifically of *malpractice*—is considered the most heinous of insults to the physician! To even suggest that one did not practice "to the utmost of his ability" is insulting . . . but to practice *below* the acceptable standard would be met with unmitigated self-condemnation and recrimination. Not being top gun is one thing; being substandard is entirely different! The insinuation elicits a feeling of humiliation—one's very integrity has been questioned.

This basic "standard of care" is inherent in the daily practice of medicine. Even a simple inference about *malpractice* will generate considerable anger in the physician. Such insinuations hurt the proud physician to the very quick. There are few true "rules" in the practice of medicine. There is little need for specific statutes. Integrity has served for centuries as the unwritten law and directing force for medical care.

Yes, malpractice is indeed a terribly serious accusation. It is in no way as serious or offensive, however, as is the suggestion of NEGLIGENCE! The very term intensifies the accusation beyond words. Herein lies the ultimate insult and damnation. If malpractice is the venial sin, then negligence is truly the cardinal sin. Let there be no mistake about it: This is absolutely the most degrading, insulting accusation a physician can encounter. It is human to make a mistake; an erroneous diagnosis, an improper choice of treatment, or simply an error in judgment may occur at times. No one performs at "max" all of the time, but we should not confuse this with credibility in regard to honor and integrity. It is by no means *negligence* simply to have erred in one's judgment. It can be, but not necessarily. The error might well imply malpractice if it was quite obvious and so basic that most physicians would readily recognize it as being substandard care. This type of blatant error is precisely what malpractice insurance is designed to "cover." If an obvious mistake—for instance, a judgmental error that competent physicians would not ordinarily make—*has* been committed, then perhaps some type of compensation may be in order, but only if the error caused harm to the patient. That is the very principle of insurance, be it automobile insurance, disability insurance, or for that matter any catastrophic insurance. *Compensation for injury or loss* is something almost everyone favors. This "damage" may occur in medicine, and when it does, a compensation to the injured party may well be in order. This is a far cry, however, from *negligence.* This chapter deals with the specific effect malpractice has on the physician.

The very first law of medicine is one well known to all health care professionals: *non primum nocere* (above all, do no harm). It does not say anything about curing all people. That would be extremely unrealisitic. Recognition of this frailty and limitation is a source of great solace to physicians because they will not cure everyone.

The admission that we as physicians are human and cannot be expected to be perfect requires reiteration. It must be an accepted fact in every patient/physician "contract." We *will do no harm*—but our mortal imperfections must be an acceptable risk to the patient. Yes, I think I am a good physician (and I hope a very good physician), but I am not the very best physician. I cannot be top gun at all times, forever. There are many doctors who know more facts than I, and there are many doctors who might take slightly "better care" of a patient on occasion. That again is part of the top-gun theory. No Olympic decathlon competitor can give his very best performance time after time and remain top gun for very long. I *can* take care of you, however; I want to take good care of you; and I *will* take good care of you. But, most importantly, *non primum nocere.* In fact, I shall take extremely good care of you. As "good" as anyone can who is in a clinical practice. This care, however, may not always be *perfect.* I sincerely hope that it will be, but I cannot guarantee it. Some days, this care may be a little bit better than others. Some days, even the top gun may fly better than other days. There are no guarantees—only the promise that, to the best of my ability, I shall not harm you and I shall do my best to help you. Medical care has inherent risks, and the only physician who has *no* complications is the one who provides *no* care. An integral part of the patient/physician "contract" includes this implied consent: No harm will be done (knowingly) and no result can be guaranteed. This is an unwritten contract between us *mortals* (physicians and patients).

There are inherent risks to certain procedures and treatments, and the risk of injury unfortunately becomes a real statistic on occasion. This should not necessarily be construed as "harm." If a physician delivers several thousand babies, statistically there will be several neonatal deaths in this group. This may be the result of complications such as premature delivery, infection, or congenital anomaly (malformation). This does not imply that the physician caused any of these abnormalities. Yes, he *could* have caused them, and if he did, then certainly this should be addressed. The physician is indeed accountable for this. All physicians would agree wholeheartedly with this concept of accountability. In the absence of negligence, however, the physician should not be held responsible for an outcome. *Accountability* does not imply *responsibility*. Responsibility implies cause and effect; accountability does not. The physician should be incriminated only if negligence was involved—not because of a "mal-result."

Something quite different is currently in vogue. The physician, especially the obstetrician, is being incriminated whenever the result of a delivery is less than 100 percent of that expected. This responsibility may be the result of consumerism (having unrealistic expectations), capitalization (attempting to gain monetary remuneration for the patient and her attorney), or of frustration (from experiencing anything less than the desired outcome). The physician is still being held liable regardless of the cause. This is the "rub." This feeling—this unrelenting persecution—is pervasive throughout medicine today. It is the primary reason so many obstetricians are abandoning their practices. This subltle but constant anxiety is truly intolerable. The part of this equation that is the most disturbing is the fact that in spite of good medical care—specifically, in the absence of negligence—several enormous judgments have been made against some outstanding physicians. When practicing good medicine is no longer a satisfactory defense against being sued, the physician has been rendered defenseless.

The unwritten patient/physician contract mentioned previously has certain advantages for the patient. The physician does guarantee that whatever is done will be absolutely in the patient's best interest. That is, the patient must always come first, above all else (fame, fortune, convenience, whatever). It does not matter that it could be 3 A.M., New Year's Eve, a wedding anniversary, or that the physician may prefer to be performing other activities. The physician is committed to the patient by this unwritten contract. He or a designated associate will not

49

abandon you no matter how complicated or extensive the illness may be. He may need to seek consultation, but he will not abandon you, and he will be with you through "thick and thin"—regardless.

The feature that makes this patient/physician relationship so unique is the fact that the physician's personal gain is, by design, not a consideration. Wouldn't it be reassuring and comforting if we never had to worry about someone's personal, vested interest in a "deal"? When sales commissions and profits are involved in business transactions, people tend to lose their objectivity. The classic example is the prototypical salesman. I am in no way disparaging salesmen—I am simply referring to the potential hazards and jeopardy involved in such transactions. This jeopardy and the apprehension are simply not a consideration in medicine. They would be in direct violation of the basic code of ethics in medicine.

Perhaps this single fact explains why so many physicians fall prey to "sucker deals." Doctors are notoriously known to be poor "business people" and exhibit poor judgment in financial endeavors. They enter transactions with a very naïve attitude, and they tend to take things at face value. The fact that salesmanship may be involved in "deals" is a concept that is somewhat foreign to the physician. Physicians learn ethics in medical school as an integral part of their training. Salesmanship is never a consideration. The physician provides *necessary* services—he or she does not sell things. This serves to reiterate that there should be no salesmanship in the practice of medicine. Salesmanship is unnecessary; it owes its existence to consumerism. This explains why the majority of practicing physicians are so averse to advertising in medicine. There is little need for salesmanship as long as integrity remains the principal prerequisite for practicing medicine.

Because of such a commitment to honor and integrity, any suggestion or inference of malpractice, especially negligence, arouses the physicians's anger. Anger in this case arises out of feeling betrayed and hurt—betrayed because the physician-patient alliance has been broken and an adversarial relationship has taken its place. The physician feels hurt because his or her pride is shattered to think a patient might feel "harmed." I can accept not curing everybody—but to have done someone harm! This cause-and-effect type of guilt is extremely threatening to any physician. No physician would willfully harm a patient. The Ethics Committee and the State Board of Medical Examiners should revoke the license of any physician who willfully harms a patient. Almost every county and state medical society has an ethics and grievance committee for the said purpose of reviewing any complaints of this nature.

A word about ethics is warranted at this point. Unethical behavior in medical practice is as despicable as negligence. It does not carry the legal ramifications that malpractice does, but it is equally disgusting. Ethics is a distinctive feature of medicine. This moral code must be adhered to explicitly if the medical profession is to continue to be afforded the esteem bestowed upon it. The final chapter in this book is dedicated to deriving an approach to quality assurance and ethics as well as a feasible solution to the malpractice crisis. Suffice it to say, though, that as far as physicians are concerned, negligence and unethical behavior are somewhat equivalent: neither is acceptable in *any* way.

Anger is a very prominent feature of every malpractice suit. The physician's honor and dignity are threatened; integrity is being questioned. Anger is an easier emotion to accept than is humiliation; so rather than cry, it is more acceptable to become angry. Certainly, depression is an inseparable part of the reaction to such accusations, but anger remains the principal emotion exhibited.

I can certainly relate to the anger generated in alleged cases of malpractice. In my only personal encounter with such an allegation, I remember my initial disappointment and anguish at the discovery of such an accusation. Even though I knew full well that there was absolutely no negligence involved, I was extremely perturbed. I became enraged upon reading the summons. The "expert witness" who was *employed* by the plaintiff's attorney was not even a practicing physician, but rather a typical "hired gun." He had testified in numerous malpractice cases, and he was, by reputation, a "drifter," having lived in at least three different states over a short period of time. He certainly was not a normal, respected practicing physician, and his accusations were totally false and inaccurate. Nonetheless, the anger aroused was quite powerful. Even the method of notification is an insult to a practicing physician. A subpoena is issued to the doctor in his office by a sheriff's deputy. Perhaps I am a little paranoid, but I found it demeaning to have a summons delivered by "the law" as if I were a rank-and-file criminal.

I must recount my first recollection of a malpractice suit because I think it typifies the reaction that people (physicians included) experience. I was doing my obstetrics and gynecology residency training when I became aware of a malpractice suit against a local psychiatrist in practice. I knew absolutely no specifics of the suit, so my impressions were based solely on media coverage and public sentiment and totally unbiased by fact! My first impression, with absolutely no knowledge per se, was that obviously some substandard care must have been involved or a suit would not have been filed in the first place. This impression was shared by many other local physicians, who, I might add, were equally uninformed. Albeit unfounded, this was the prevailing assessment.

How was such an erroneous assumption, absolutely unfounded and unsupported by fact, derived? Here I was, a physician and a colleague so to speak, and surely I should have been at least sympathetic. With no knowledge of the case, I assumed some guilt by the very nature of the accusation. After all, medical jurisprudence is based upon retribution or reparation of some *harm,* is it not? Surely a suit would not have been filed had there not been just cause. WRONG! Incredible as it may seem, all it takes to file a suit is to find or employ an "expert witness" who will attest to the fact that some substandard of care was provided. Obviously, it also requires an unhappy patient (or family member) and a plaintiff attorney. Unfortunately, there are just a few of both around. We as physicians are to blame for the unhappy patient. Perhaps society is to blame for the glut of plaintiff attorneys who are only too happy to accommodate a client and submit a suit for almost any damage alleged to have arisen from malpractice. Neither of these two resultant developments was by primary design, but we must each accept responsibility.

This "expert" is oftentimes a self-proclaimed expert because the term is without specific definition. It would be much more apropos simply to call this person a witness because all too often he is certainly not an expert in any sense of the word—especially not in clinical medicine. His livelihood may depend upon his testimony, so he certainly cannot be considered an unbiased witness. The point here is simply that the initiation of the suit requires only that *some* physician is willing to swear in court that malpractice (defined as substandard care) was committed. In recently reevaluating my previous reaction to this suit, I realized I was prejudiced *against* my colleague. I was somewhat embarrassed by this, so I decided to question several current contemporaries about their initial experience with this suit, as best they remembered it. I inquired (1) if they remembered anything about the suit (which had occurred more than 15 years ago) and (2) if they had any "negative" impressions concerning the defendant doctor.

Most of the physicians queried did remember the suit. No specific details were required to answer this affirmatively. The response to the part concerning negative feelings is most interesting. Without exception, every single physician responded that they attributed some guilt to the defendant physician as represented by the fact that everyone questioned felt some wrongdoing must have provoked the initiation of the suit! Their recollections were as totally unwarranted and without documentation as mine had been. Just as my initial impression had been based on intuition and not fact, my colleagues were victims of a similar innate feeling that some "wrong" had been perpetrated. All of this, mind you, was devoid of fact. It was simply emotion. Ultimately, the psychiatrist was finally acquitted in the case. It is now almost 20 years later, and our same negative feelings (unfounded incrimination of the psychiatrist) persist. This feeling is held by *fellow* physicians who one might think would normally "identify" with the psychiatrist and the process and not incriminate a contemporary simply because he was the "victim" of a lawsuit. Yet even fellow physicians condemn the accused, and it does not make one bit of difference whether he is innocent or not. He loses by the nature of an accusation. This astounds me. It is a no-win situation all over again! Only in medical jurisprudence are you considered *guilty* until proved *innocent*. In this particular case, the psychiatrist was exonerated; yet he still suffers the stigma of having "gotten away with something." In reality, though, he did no wrong whatsoever. Even your peers assume you are guilty whenever a suit is filed—not lost, merely filed.

I cannot explain the complex psychology responsible for local physicians' consistent replies when questioned about that first law suit. Was it contempt for the doctor? Was it simply prejudice against any defendant in a lawsuit? Even the acquittal was accompanied by feelings or implications that the physician was in some way guilty of something. If physicians themselves assume such guilt associated with a medical/legal suit, we can imagine what the lay public must think. I have yet to find any positive event that arises from involvement in *any* suit. A "tie" would be a blessing. If this suit is any indication, a physician cannot even attain a "tie" when he wins. He cannot "break even" or come away unscathed 20 years later even though he may well be perfectly innocent. Is this stigma of guilt fair? What happened to an individual's rights and the adage "innocent till proven guilty?" This simple legal courtesy is allowed even the most ardent of common criminals. Surely physicians should at least rank up there with the best of these rogues.

One of the contributing factors in the lawyers/doctors controversy has its evolution in the training programs to which each professional is subjected. The educational background of each is diametrically opposed. Medical school is replete with ethics and integrity. That is not to say that law school is not concerned with these principles, but they are certainly not the primary objective. One of the primary objectives in law school is to learn how to defend and/or protect your client. It goes without saying that lawyers may on occasion be defending someone who is "guilty," and it then becomes their duty or challenge (or whatever justification one chooses) to defend their client to the fullest. I am not certain, morally, whether this should include "getting them off" on a technicality. I have difficulty accepting this principle. By finding some "loophole" in the law, a lawyer may then win a case, and these tactics are not only readily acceptable, but deemed laudable. After all, an attorney is supposed to defend his or her client to the utmost, and that means doing anything within his or her power (legally) to aid and abet the cause. Improve the outcome at all costs! Manipulating the law is considered part of the art, and the more skilled the lawyer, the more adept he or she is at this.

When you have done something wrong, don't you want the "best" lawyer to defend you? And who is the the best? The lawyer who can get you "off" even when you are guilty!

Attorneys deal strictly with the law—not morality. Moral obligation is absolutely worthless in a court of law—statutes rule. Technicalities can be all-important. A man can literally kill someone, and if his rights (even as a hard-core criminal) are violated, he can have his conviction nullified even though he is guilty beyond any shadow of a doubt. His status is changed to "not guilty." This type of manipulation of the law was responsible for a very good friend of mine withdrawing from law school after the first year. Because his unquestioned integrity was violated by the principle of winning at all costs, he found it unacceptable to continue. His values would not be compromised.

My friend with integrity contrasts markedly with the Florida lawyer who has quite a reputation for getting drunk drivers acquitted in spite of their obvious guilt. He supposedly has had 1,100 (!) consecutive acquittals of drunk drivers without losing a single case. This was accomplished through manipulation of the law through legal technicalities. This "gentleman" takes great pride in finding such loopholes in the law, with full knowledge that his clients were absolutely, unquestionably guilty. Guilty was just redefined: not guilty. After all, it is just a legal definition. In a television interview ("60 Minutes") this attorney alluded to the fact that his ability to "get them off" was simply part of the price we pay for a democracy.

If you are a drunk driver cited in South Florida, you will certainly want the "best" lawyer to defend you. When the "best" is in reality actually the *worst* for society, something is dreadfully wrong with the system.

The educational background of most attorneys contributes to some of the difficulty in medical jurisprudence. Lawyers simply do not relate to how degrading and insulting it is to be named a defendant in a malpractice suit. Their training centers on adversarial relationships, whereas just the initiation of a medical malpractice suit insinuates something that is totally contrary to the very principle so often stressed throughout medical school: Above all, do no harm.

The situation involving the physician-lawyer conflict is further compounded by the nature of the legal system itself. Winning is paramount. Principle frequently has little to do with the final outcome in many suits. All too often, lawyers will weigh all of the evidence and evaluate the facts, and then in actuality have no earthly idea whether a case will be won or lost once it goes to litigation. The outcome will be based on the interpretation of these facts. Furthermore, although the actual principles involved in a case may be rather clear, how a jury will interpret and react to them is totally unpredictable. The oft-quoted cliché, "It will be up to the jury," holds true. Shouldn't something so complex and important be determined by those having considerable knowledge about the subject—that is, a panel of true experts? How can a jury be expected to know enough medicine to judge a physician —especially when self-proclaimed medical "experts" are employed by both sides to educate these very jurors? There must be a better, more equitable system.

Furthermore, attorneys for the plaintiff frequently admit that their principal weapon in a malpractice case is their ability to establish a lack of credibility on the defendant physician's part. Irrespective of the quality of medicine practiced, if the doctor's sincerity or credibility can be dented, there is a tremendous chance that the jury may be swayed in favor of the plaintiff. If the plaintiff's attorney can create any suspicion of insensitivity or indifference on the physician's part, causation of injury is almost irrelevant. Theatrics abound! But what happened to the *facts!* Trial lawyers readily admit the facts become secondary. The personal affront is perfectly acceptable. Even though it may have nothing to do with the actual medicine practiced, it will certainly have something to do with how the jury interprets the case. Nor is this unique to medical/legal issues. Trial lawyers employ this tactic as one of the principal weapons in their armamentarium. Establish a crack in someone's credibility, and the case is essentially won.

There is agreement among physicians that considerable negligent behavior exists in medicine. In fact, some of this negligent behavior is so offensive as literally to cause shame to the medical profession. There is some quite terrible medicine practiced in this country, indeed. Fortunately, not much, but *any* is too much. A point in fact is that there are some rather contemptible physicians. There is no doubt that this unacceptable behavior must be dealt with and in a most stringent manner.

Unfortunately, the present medical/legal system does not even address the problem. The current medical/legal system is merely a form of a monetary compensation. It is a system of dollar reparations rather than a system dealing specifically with the quality of medical care. Reparations could better be served by an accident type of insurance policy, without regard for causation. In truly negligent cases, more education, supervision, and physician reprimands are in order—not monetary remuneration in inordinate amounts to a patient. Enormous awards do little to deter malpractice. Tremendous awards only encourage more suits. It is wrong merely to pay enormous sums of money through an insurance provision and have the offending physician walk away unscathed. That hardly addresses the problem of negligent behavior. If a physician is truly guilty of malpractice (negligence), then the discipline should include an appropriate reprimand, not just an enormous economic windfall for the patient. The present system does nothing to prevent recurrences; it only compensates the plaintiff and his or her lawyer. The point here is that sincere physicians are very concerned about negligent behavior, and we welcome a system to help curb such loathsome behavior. The current system does nothing to correct this problem.

To illustrate further the discrepancy between lawyers' and physicians' philosophies, let us look at their attitudes toward a lawsuit. Physicians are often told by the defense lawyer, as well as on occasion by the plaintiff lawyer, "Do not take it personally." A lawyer expressed this to me in a slightly different vein by saying that *he* was not suing anyone personally, but rather he was only suing for his client. The lawyer simply represented the client. I can attest to the fact that *any* physician takes it extremely personally when he or she is sued! It infers an accusation of gross negligence—an insult to the physician's integrity. This degradation is insurmountable and terribly personal. The ultimate insult is to be accused of practicing substandard medicine. What a horrible crime to practice poor medicine or, worse yet, harmful medicine. Bringing such a lawsuit may be considered just part of the job to a lawyer, but it is absolutely disruptive to the physician. Accusations about the quality of a doctor's surgery or about life-and-death decisions he has made are serious. Very serious. A lawyer's cavalier attitude about being sued is undeniably offensive. Would a judge consider a question about his honesty as serious or personal?

The emotional reaction to being named in a suit is something no physician is prepared for. You are served a summons or may receive a registered letter—totally unexpectedly and almost invariably right in the middle of a busy day. You are rendered functionless by a feeling of total devastation. It is the most supreme insult imaginable. You feel as though you have been totally betrayed by the patient.

My initial reaction was rather typical. I was hardly able to see another patient for the remainder of that afternoon. Maybe I shall lose my license. Maybe a jury will not understand the case, and I could be found guilty in spite of my innocence. After all, it would not be the first time that this has happened. Panic begins to set in. All of a sudden, it is not simply a matter of enjoying the practice of medicine: It is survival. My family's livelihood depends upon my vocation. Even though I did nothing wrong, I know full well that enormous settlements and/or awards have been made in spite of good medical care. This wholly unfair system now threatens my existence. Utter despair soon replaces exasperation. Only the discovery of an unexpected case of spousal infidelity could cause as much emotional upheaval as being served a medical/legal summons. Physicians have known for a long time that the system is extremely unfair. Now I am a victim of this very system!

The ever-present fear of being sued is so prevalent today that every physician literally cringes when there is any complication in a patient's care. This anxiety is predominant, irrespective of the cause of the complication. This paranoid, defensive posture is unwarranted, not to mention uncomfortable. There is enough stress in the routine practice of medicine without having to endure this undeserved incrimination. One mistake and you, as a physician, could live the remainder of your life a penniless pauper. Perhaps a better question would be: "Is this fair to your family?" This scenario leads physicians to alter their practice of medicine—that is, to discontinue obstetrical care. I just do not think I can bat 1,000! I do not mind trying, but I am not perfect. I cannot afford to play the game if one error means total destruction.

After receiving the summons concerning the malpractice suit against me, I cannot remember how long it took to sleep through a night without being awakened because of anxiety. The anxiety invariably elicited anger—yet, I had done nothing wrong! That provided little consolation. A patient had a gastrointestinal disease which ultimately resulted in a complication, but the patient (via her attorney) was alleging that our surgery had actually caused the complication. Even though we knew there was no negligence involved, the personal distress aroused by the suit was immeasurable. I am firmly convinced that neither the patient nor the mercenary "expert witness" who was consulted truly felt that *negligence* was involved, but this fact had little to do with deterring them from filing suit. Perhaps it was hoped that some monetary gain might come from such an action. Besides, there is absolutely no deterrent to filing such a suit other than having to pay an "expert" to render an opinion. Once an "expert witness" has been employed, it is simply a matter of typing up a form and "off" you go. "Ready access" to the courts for lawsuits does little to deter frivolous claims.

The mental anguish is immeasurable. The initial reaction to a suit is an emotional experince long remembered. Any physician who has experienced it—and seven out of every ten obstetricians has—readily admits how very *painful* it is. The frustration is terrible; you are rendered helpless. It is almost pathetic to be so ravaged. It is an emotion few people should ever have to endure. The breach of trust—the patient/physician relationship—is the most painful disappointment. Even if you expected to be sued for a bad outcome, I actually suppose receiving the summons would elicit the same response. You might suspect your spouse of being unfaithful, for example, but then to be confronted with the fact itself must still be a traumatic experience.

This betrayal by the patient is very demoralizing. Years of medical training toward excellence only serve to make physicians very critical of their own work. Only a minister can be more concerned with how the public perceives his intentions. For a physician to suffer such a tremendous insult as being named a "defendant" and to feel so rejected create a loneliness that is almost frightening. You cannot and do not want to tell anyone. Not colleagues, not family, not friends. Because physicians have such obsessive/compulsive personalities, their self-esteem is so damaged that they begin to wonder seriously if they have indeed been negligent. Do I practice sloppy medicine? Even if I don't, everyone will now certainly think that I do. Should I have done something differently?

What despair! There is absolutely no way to glean anything positive from being sued. Every physician knows this—*no* attorney does.

In a profession where integrity and honor represent the very essence of one's existence, being involved in a lawsuit is definitely a losing proposition. Because attorneys can take a "bad case" in which someone is guilty and have him acquitted on technicalities, they can "win" a case in spite of facts to the contrary. Integrity and honor, even "right" and "wrong," do not dictate what happens in this legal system. There is no premium on intent or ethics. If an attorney can find a statute or a precedent, he can win regardless of the issue in question. Technicalities and slick expertise determine far too many decisions in the courtroom. And to think that my fate might now be decided by such theatrics.

Moral issues are not even a consideration in most cases. It is strictly a matter of interpretation of the law. This total independence from moral issues is extremely confusing to the physician. A lawsuit, even a frivolous one, is considered an awful blemish on a physician's reputation. Few people outside the medical profession realize how fragile a physician's image can be, especially to him as a person. The obsessive-compulsive personality is quick to blame himself even in the absence of just cause. As previously mentioned, only a minister or perhaps a politician is more acutely aware of his reputation. Your fellow physicians believe that being sued means that you "lose." The mentality that prevails is this: "You must have done *something* wrong to be sued in the first place!"

Reassurance is sorely needed. Life cannot be as miserable as you feel it is during that first week. Repeatedly, I asked myself the question: "*Is* my practice substandard?" There is an immediate sense of helplessness, anxiety, and depression, no matter how frivolous that suit. Consciously and subconsciously, you begin to question your ability; you lose all sense of confidence. Suddenly, you suffer the indignity of ingratitude at having performed medical service well for many years. Years of practicing "perfect" medicine are now meaningless. What a waste! In addition to the depression, there is an indescribable bitterness over being sued. That the law suit represents one patient out of thousands matters very little. A once benevolent attitude is suddenly replaced with a vengeance which is almost frightening. The embarrassment and the shame are competing emotions with an intense anger. The anxiety is totally consuming in the beginning. There are repeated episodes of overt hostility. You will mentally "quit" your practice several hundred times a day during those first few weeks. You rehearse many times what you will say to the patient when you are confronted at your next encounter. All of the wonderful things you have done—the "saves" to your credit—offer little solace. Besides, no one will even know about those. Society can be rather unforgiving: You save hundreds of lives, help hundreds of people, and no one knows you, but rob one bank. . . . The reaction to this anger frequently results in some irrational behavior. Quarreling with one's family, the desire to countersue, the desire to leave the profession, even suicide—all are considered over and over again. This could easily be the most traumatic event in one's life, and to think it could be just a frivolous suit!

A succinct article from *Medical Economics,* a contemporary medical periodical, is presented unabridged.[1] It says a great deal about the entire situation in a rather brief report.

> Thanksgiving preparations in suburban Woodbury, Long Island, were shadowed last Nov. 25 by the death of a physician who had served the community for more than a quarter of a century. Sitting at his desk in his modest home-office, he wrote his wife a terse note, then injected himself with a lethal dose of morphine and meperidine.
>
> The 72-year-old general practitioner, George F. Laszlo, had been sued for malpractice the previous year; the trial had been set for last Nov. 19 and then abruptly rescheduled for January.

Friends and family consider his death a consequence of the post-ponement as much as the lawsuit itself.

On principle, Laszlo had practiced bare of liability insurance. "He hated the way people used malpractice suits to enrich themselves," explains his son, George A. Laszlo, a corporate consultant in information management. "My father felt that the litigious malpractice climate was aiding and abetting people's worst motives. His way of fighting that was to refuse to carry liability insurance. His death was a final act of non-participation—the ultimate checking out." In 1985, during his fifth decade in practice, Laszlo had received a summons from the Supreme Court of Nassau County, informing him that he'd been accused of medical malpractice by a longtime patient. According to Laszlo's defense attorney, Raymond J. Furey of Hempstead, N.Y., the doctor recalled advising the 55-year-old man to go to the hospital. The patient refused, and subsequently suffered a heart attack. His suit blamed Laszlo for failure to diagnose and treat a heart condition.

"The summons came as a great shock," says Furey. "He felt the suit had no merit. When I met with Dr. Laszlo to prepare for the trial, he seemed confident of the medical facts of the case, while concerned about his financial vulnerability."

Laszlo suffered a small stroke, resulting in right-side paralysis, in July 1986. "My mother and I blame the stress of the lawsuit," says his son. "But my father recovered about 90 percent. He fought off depression and managed to psyche himself up for the trial. He was articulate and never shy in front of an audience. He was eager to refute the charges and put the trial behind him before the new year. The week that he died, he was anticipating having surgery to remove his gallbladder."

General surgeon Joseph Bennett, a close friend for 20 years, concurs. "He had girded himself for Nov. 19, but once the case was postponed, he had to renew his strength. In retrospect, I think that was too much for him.

"George had always shown tremendous enthusiasm for life," he recalls. "Then, during the past year, with the suit pending and his assets vulnerable, I saw his spirits fall. I could still engage him in good conversation. But I sensed he was distant from me.

What Malpractice Means to the Physician

When I'd ask what was bothering him, he'd tell me it was the malpractice litigation."

Still, the doctor's suicide took Bennett and others by surprise. "He'd been through tough times before," says his son. "He'd immigrated from Hungary to America alone and earned his license to practice here before bringing my mother, sister, and me over. He brought his parents over, too, and supported them until their deaths. I didn't think that after all that he'd be done in by a lawsuit he considered frivolous."

In retrospect, surgeon Bennett wishes he'd implored his anxious friend "not to become a victim of the tort system he hated." In their talks, Laszlo had confided his disillusionment with the litigiousness of contemporary American society. "He felt patients and attorneys sued physicians mostly for material gain," Bennett recalls. "He couldn't understand mercenary desires. He found his pleasure in history, music, travel, and art—not in money."

Laszlo had gone bare for those philosophical reasons, but Bennett says he also had practical ones: "He worked alone, he was very thorough, he didn't hesitate to refer patients to a consultant."

Laszlo and his wife, Maritza, 66, formerly a film actress and classical singer in her native Hungary, lived in the split-level house he'd purchased in 1961, three years after he'd arrived in Brooklyn, N.Y., to take courses to qualify for his New York license. In Hungary he'd worked for 20 years as a radiologist and surgeon, but decided to practice in the U.S. as a G.P.

Laszlo worked out of his Woodbury home. In later years, with an eye to retirement, he started cutting back his 60-plus weekly practice hours to four days a week, taking no new patients. He also began a casual search for a younger colleague to take over.

As he cut back his hours, Laszlo immersed himself more than ever in his main hobby, a comprehensive history of the world that he'd begun in his teens. "He thought conventional history was too narrow," says his son. "He felt he'd drawn some original conclusions. He was seeing the forest, not just the trees as most historians do. Working on his history was really the only thing that distracted him from the malpractice case."

When the trial was postponed to January, defense attorney Furey phoned Laszlo with the news, citing its cause: The plaintiff was too ill to attend. "I've worried that there was something more I should have said and didn't," Furey muses now. "But Dr. Laszlo didn't seem depressed to me. And I wonder sometimes whether he thought that by killing himself he would put an end to the lawsuit against his estate. He didn't, you know; the trial will proceed."

Indeed, says Furey, the trial is now set for this month, after yet another postponement. The plaintiff died in April, and there's talk of changing the malpractice charge to wrongful death. "Laszlo's suicide," the doctor's attorney adds, "won't even be an issue."

Six days after the first postponement, as he prepared to inject himself with narcotics, Laszlo wrote these few words his wife would read upon her return from a concert: "No one should feel guilt for my doing this. I've had a good life, and you've all been good to me. But it's not enough."[1]

The most disheartening part of the article is the total disregard for this physician's emotions. Only the physician subjected to suit can tell you what "pain and suffering" represent. It seems ironic that it is the plaintiff who is suing for so much money because of pain and suffering. Payment for pain and suffering might be terribly expensive if the persecuted physician's emotion could be quantified and the appropriate reparation made. This is especially true in lawsuits not having true merit. What a travesty of justice. The more conscientious the physician, the more tumultuous the emotional upheaval—despite a suit's triviality.

"Don't be so upset by a lawsuit." "Don't take it personally." "It's no 'big deal.'" Sure. You bet. Good luck! I know one physician who became so embittered because of a malpractice suit that his entire personality changed. He subsequently divorced his wife of some 20 years, and his usually jovial, kind manner was replaced by a cautious, suspicious, almost pensive attitude. Such changes are in no way uncommon after such an emotional upheaval.

The subpoena may just as well have included the wife's name—

and probably the children's also. The entire family is involved from the outset. Even when a protective father tries initially to spare his family disgrace, the anger and bitterness which are generated by the suit eventually surface. Birthdays, funerals, weddings, and holidays do not allow any reprieve. The suit invariably makes its way into the newspapers. It is frequently on TV. Newsworthy facts usually continue to be discussed for years. Since the average suit requires five to seven years to complete, you must be prepared for years of adverse press. Everything associated with the suit will be detrimental to you, and even the thought of a vacation generates tremendous animosity and anger. There is simply no escaping it—the lawsuit permeates all facets of your life.

The medical marriage is truly tested by a medical malpractice suit. A small rift may easily become the Grand Canyon. Many suits go beyond the limits of one's liability coverage, and this threatens the family's future. Economic stability is in jeopardy. Most medical families remember all too well the early years of heavy debt and the uphill struggle to gain financial independence. The threat of losing everything is terribly unnerving. How can anyone survive being threatened with the fact that they may be literally millions of dollars in debt because of one allegedly errant medical decision. It is a frightening thought to consider that one decision—even one made in good faith—could result in total financial and emotional disaster. The decision may have been a correct one according to the accepted standard of care, but if a "maloccurrence" resulted, you can still lose the case even though you were not negligent. God forbid that you should ever make the wrong decision! It is most amazing to me, as an individual, that such an absurd system continues to be tolerated. It is absolutely unreasonable.

I thought that protection was the purpose of the large insurance premiums physicians must pay. The pressure never to make a mistake becomes unbearable. Forget personal humiliation—think only of the stress. Changing your entire life based on one decision is stressful enough, but to think that your entire family's welfare could be in jeopardy for that same decision produces more pressure than most people are willing to accept. The shame and the "hurt" associated with a lawsuit are also family affairs. Imagine someone saying that your spouse is an absolutely unfit person in his or her profession, claiming that he or she is "grossly negligent" and is guilty of substandard practices. The guilt the children are subjected to is extremely unfair; kids can be awfully cruel. The shame, embarrassment, and humiliation associated with being sued, publicly, is all part of the guilt shared by the entire family. These injustices result just because the physician *is sued,* not because he loses or wins the suit.

Because the social, financial, and professional status a doctor enjoys is so threatened by a suit, is it any wonder that being sued has been equated with discovering that one has a terminal (fatal) illness? Five to seven years is an exceedingly long period of time. It hardly seems fair to persecute one's entire family for such an extended length of time. Certainly a more expeditious system would benefit all concerned. A more equitable system allowing a quick settlement might eliminate some of the legal fees involved in the continuous banter over issues between the two opposing sides. Besides, why should anyone be concerned with the physician or his family's emotions since they are of no concern to anyone "personally"? Is it any wonder, then, that the stress factor in obstetrics is insurmountable? Can you imagine functioning in a system where one alleged error in judgment can wreck such havoc? Neurologically impaired infants (brain-damaged infants) frequently result in multi-million-dollar settlements. This certainly exceeds the normal liability coverage and directly threatens a physician's financial security. To function in such a system, one obviously desires insurance. In the state of Georgia currently a $1,000,000 insurance policy costs approximately $60,000 per year. If an obstetrician elects to deliver only 5 babies a month, he must charge $1,000 per patient just to cover the malpractice premium.

Let us imagine, if you will, the example of an infant born with cerebral palsy. There are numerous cases of this happening, and in the vast majority of these (probably 90 percent) the delivery process has absolutely nothing to do with the *cause* of the impairment. Nevertheless, there are numerous instances in which proper, good medicine has been practiced, yet enormous settlements have been made. Equally disturbing is the fact that these awards—perhaps *rewards*—have been for sums of money far in excess of anyone's insurance coverage. The magnitude of the awards is frightening. This stress factor is the most important problem facing obstetrics today. Most physicians will not continue to face this stress without some modification in their behavior.

To eliminate such potentially disastrous circumstances, young obstetricians are abandoning obstetrics in droves. I did. If practicing good medicine is not adequate protection against malpractice liability, then one is rendered defenseless. Under the current system, it is simply a matter of time before one will become a victim of circumstance. If for no other reason, your family should be spared this jeopardy. The liability may be economic, social, emotional, or physical—or, all of these.

Obstetrics, a medical specialty in which you can only play for a *tie,* is certainly frustrating; but to play and always *lose* is absolutely unacceptable.

NOTES

1. Brown, S., The Doctor Who Chose Death Over a Malpractice Trial, Medical Economics, June 22, 1987; 73.

CHAPTER 5

Abuse of the Tort Law System

IT IS FORTUNATE INDEED that the tort law system exists. Under the tort law system, if a civil wrong is committed, an action can be filed in court to recover monetary damages for any injury resulting from negligent acts or intentional misconduct. Were it not for the tort system, angry patients or their families might be stalking physicians on the street with a club in hand. The medical profession is totally in favor of *due process:* the legal procedure that has been established in a system of jurisprudence for the enforcement and protection of private rights. Simply stated, it means a fair trial, due process, or "your day in court." All physicians readily endorse this concept. Recognizing their fallibility, physicians themselves sought a system of insurance for possible inadvertent but wrongful acts. Carrying insurance in case of possible calamity is nothing new. Actually, there is little wrong with either the tort system or the insurance system, conceptually. The problem is solely one of implementation. The monetary remuneration in this system has become almost obscene! Once again, money is the root of all evil. It is the awards—perhaps more appropriately called *rewards*—that now threaten the very system itself. The system that was originally designed to redress grievances has now become a system of monetary reparation for any injury, irrespective of cause.

It is very easy to see why advertising on TV, etc., has become so popular with many young plaintiff attorneys. If awards are so astronomically high (and I think $65 million, for example, falls in this category!), it could take literally only one case of medical malpractice to make an attorney a fabulously wealthy individual. What is perhaps even more alarming is the fact that such large settlements might stem from an imperfect result rather than from negligence.

Plaintiff attorneys receive what is called a *contingency fee:* This is a fee agreement between the plaintiff and the plaintiff's attorney whereby the plaintiff agrees to pay the attorney a percentage of all damages recovered for an injury. This fee is independent of the amount of time and effort put into the case, because it is strictly a percentage of the settlement. This figure is typically 35 to 40 percent of the total award in medical malpractice cases. In a case which might be settled for $2.5 million, a plaintiff lawyer would receive $1 million (40 percent). This might easily be a case that involved an error in judgment or perhaps an improper or unsuccessful procedure. In such a case, settlement "out of court" could well be reached, and precious little time and energy would be required of the plaintiff attorney. From such a scenario, it becomes obvious why attorneys would advertise to review—*free of charge*—any grievance that a patient might have regarding an injury, serious illness, a retarded child, or any outcome deemed unacceptable. It is somewhat akin to a lawyer baiting many fishing lines hoping that occasionally he will *catch* the "big one." It takes only one or two "discoveries" to make an attorney a rich man. The more lines he has out, the greater the chances of a big catch.

Few people realize how simple it is to file a malpractice suit. The legal prerequisites for a medical malpractice grievance are:

1. A patient-physician relationship must exist.
2. An injury must occur.
3. The medical "standard of care" was not practiced (that is, there was substandard care).
4. The injury was *caused* by the violation of the standard of care.

Just as the tort law system itself, by definition, is good, so are the official prerequisites for a suit. No physician opposes them, and, in fact, we support them wholeheartedly. The problem lies in their interpretation and implementation. Legally, the prerequisites are excellent criteria, but how they are abused!

In reality, any patient who is less than pleased with a "result" can consult an attorney and attempt to file a lawsuit. As everyone is now aware through massive media advertising, there are myriads of eager young lawyers who will gladly review a medical record free of charge to see if some compensation might be recoverable. We live in a terribly litigious society, and this appears to be compounded by numerous activist judges who continue to expand the extent and interpretation of liability. This pervasive feeling of expanding liability has had a profound effect on the medical profession. It is now recognized by physicians that anxiety related to this liability seriously threatens the practice of medicine, especially in obstetrics. This anxiety has been responsible for the outlay of countless millions of dollars for what has become "defensive medicine." This is money spent simply "for the record" or to document something with the full knowledge that it will in no way benefit the patient.

Once an attorney reviews a medical record, the only requirement to file a suit is to find a physician—*one*—who will agree to testify that the standard of care was not met. Legally, this means "negligence" (the standard of care was not met). Do you imagine that there are certain physicians in this country who might, for a fee, attest to the fact that the standard of care was not met? Some do this without even thoroughly reviewing the chart. Oftentimes, these "experts" may be physicians who do not even practice medicine or who are not involved in patient care, but who testify repeatedly as a source of considerable income. For such self-proclaimed expert witnesses, testifying in medical-legal matters oftentimes constitutes such a major part of their income that this might just influence their objectivity and impartiality! There is absolutely no penalty or repercussion should such an "expert" testify to something which actually is erroneous or inaccurate. Shouldn't a substandard opinion given as testimony constitute medical malpractice? After all, the expert's opinion is entirely *premeditated* since the case in question should have been evaluated in considerable detail. This is obviously in contrast to the events that actually transpired originally in a case, because rarely does a practicing physician have the luxury of taking his time in the clinical setting. Having to make a critical, real-life decision "under fire" is one thing; having the advantage of enough time to do thorough research and leisurely ponder a set of circumstances is another. Surely a standard of care would again be in order for such important expert's opinions. Perhaps the system should have *qualified* experts rather than self-proclaimed experts, many of who might more appropriately be called "hired guns." A more equitable system using impartial, qualified investigators could provide a much more objective evaluation of the medical care in question.

Easy access to legal counsel is a nice convenience, but easy access in the initiation of a lawsuit is anything but inconsequential. The filing of a lawsuit initiates a cascade of events that result in considerable economic and pychological impact. This psychological impact to the physician (and upon his family) is one of complete devastation. (Anyone who has read Chapter 4 can empathize with the physician so accused). The economic impact of initiating a malpractice suit is no minor matter either. A considerable expense is incurred with the initiation of a suit because both an insurance company and a defense attorney are automatically involved from the suit's inception. A considerable expense is incurred by the insurance company investigating even a totally frivolous suit, and this figure is often in excess of $10,000. Legal opinions are expensive, and considerable investigation ("fact finding") must be done just to establish that a suit has little or no merit.

Because the tort system can be so terribly expensive, it is easy to understand why the insurance company may wish to "settle" rather than litigate a case, especially if the amount sought for damages is not too excessive. To many physicians' dismay, out-of-court settlement often involves the admission of guilt by inference, whereas absolutely *no* malpractice (negligence) may have been committed. An insurance company's desire to settle suits as a compromise (in fear of larger awards if litigated) can sometimes be a real source of consternation to physicians, especially obstetricians. Literally stated, it is a cop-out: a lesser dollar amount is agreed upon in order not to litigate and risk a more expensive settlement. The physician's guilt is conceded, but it is *never* established that wrong was done. This is an all too frequent ploy when a neurologically damaged infant is concerned because enormous monetary settlements can be imposed by compassionate but well-meaning juries. Emotion rather than reason is often a predominant factor in such cases. This emotion will be discussed in more detail shortly. The point here is simply that the insurance company may attempt to compromise: accepting culpability in exchange for a smaller monetary reparation. Obviously, in essence this reasoning is a form of gambling: "Should we accept culpability and pay a moderate settlement, or should we take a gamble on paying a large amount if the suit goes to a jury trial and we lose?" When something as important as my responsibility for negligence is concerned, I am not at all entertained by that fate being determined as part of an insurance company's gamble. My reputation and possibly my family's security could well be at stake. This settlement usually takes place before it is established that any negligence was involved.

Another consequence of accepting culpability as part of a compromise is the increased future insurance premiums. Most insurance companies prorate those clients for whom damages have been paid. I am not happy about accepting blame for something in which there was no guilt; conversely, I do not relish the thought of being millions of dollars in debt, either. Compromising smacks of having *sold* one's soul, but the possibility of an enormous jury award forces a physician to make such a concession. If there is a known injury and an allegedly negligent act that supposedly caused it, why is it so terribly difficult to project what the specific damages and award might be? The answer is rather obvious: It is up to the jury.

The current tort system has many inequities, but perhaps the two most blatant are the system of these excessive monetary reparations for injury, and the lawyer's contingency fee. These will be discussed together because they are an integral part of the problem in medical jurisprudence and because they are jointly destroying medicine as it exists in this country today. These contingency fees and huge awards are contributing directly to the demise of quality medical care. A true crisis exists *now!* Medical school applications in the mid-1970s were in excess of 5 applicants for each position available. This figure was down to 1.7 applicants per position for the fall class of 1987—and it is projected to be down to 1.3 applicants per position for 1988. This bespeaks a very serious problem. Many bright, aspiring young people in America no longer feel medicine is an appealing profession. What is perhaps more alarming is that 20 percent of the class accepted for the fall of 1987 *declined* their acceptance. In other words, they paid their application fees, took the medical aptitude tests, participated in the interview process, and yet ultimately declined their acceptance. The feature of this rejection that is most disturbing to me personally is that many students in this 20 percent were undoubtedly very bright, but, more importantly, they were extremely *perceptive* and recognized the present plight of medicine in the United States. When the caliber and number of applicants to medical school decline, it is only a matter of time before the quality of medical care in this country drops accordingly. This is a very ominous trend. It is hard for me to believe that this aspect of the crisis has received so little attention. This is just one more reason you must participate in helping to resolve this crisis. Your very care is dependent upon its resolution.

In spite of having the best medical care system in the world, there are three times as many medical malpractice suits in the United States as compared with any other country. The United States has better doctors, who are better trained, using better equipment, yet more malpractice lawsuits than any other country. It is a fact that only 6 percent of the world's population lives in the United States, yet 66 percent of the world's lawyers live here. Compared with Japan, there are ten times as many lawyers per capita in the United States. Is there any doubt as to why this concentration of lawyers has occurred? Further evidence of the preponderance of lawyers in the United States is the fact that 40,000 students are receiving law degrees in this country yearly.[2] There are approximately 700,000 lawyers in the United States already, and it is predicted that the figure will exceed 1 million by the year 2000. Do you think that business contracts, real estate closings, etc., will increase that substantially? Do you think that in our already litigious society lawsuits will become more prevalent? It is well known that the majority of medical malpractice cases involve young lawyers rather than the older, established lawyers. That is just what we need: more young aggressive attorneys.

This abundance of lawyers is not a primary concern for physicians, but medical jurisprudence *is* a concern for the doctor. The legal profession has its own problems. A 1985 Gallup poll revealed that only 27 percent of the public rated lawyers as having high ethical standards, compared with 67 percent for the clergy and 58 percent for doctors.[3]

The concern for doctors is medicine. And for the first time, "cost" is no longer the primary problem facing medicine, but rather professional liability has taken precedence.[4]

Under the present tort law system only about one-fourth of all medical malpractice insurance premium dollars goes to the injured party. Yes, only 28 cents on the dollar is actually received by the patient. Most of the money goes to the legal profession. This is a classically inefficient system in regard to the injured patient. The very purpose of the tort system is to provide for the injured party, yet he or she does not even receive the major part of the award. Let us at least devise a system wherein the injured party receives the lion's share of the payment. Even as inefficient as the monumental government bureaucracy is, only about one-third of the money taken in in taxes is actually required to administer the sytem. Imagine if the bureaucracy took two-thirds to administer the government, as the legal system does in medical jurisprudence. Of course, that would only mean that you would have to pay twice as much tax as you currently do! I am sure that would not alarm anyone.

The system of monetary awards is obviously very closely allied to the contingency fee: the larger the award, the larger that 33- to 40-percent (sometimes 45-percent) fee. The lawyer definitely has a vested interest in the jury award. The more theatrical the lawyer's presentation in court, the more a jury is likely to respond sympathetically. For instance, a day in the life of the afflicted patient (or a clever videotape) or physically baring the body for the jury's observation can be very moving. A very well presented, visible malady may be "worth" a tremendous sum of money when the jury is properly manipulated. Such subjective evaluation of a case is totally unfair, because depending upon the lawyer and the sympathy of the jurors, a case could generate either a windfall on one occasion or a minimal award on another—for the very same injury! I find this injustice offensive. This lottery concept should be replaced with a system based on definite standards with a set of values for specific inuries. There is a similar set of standards for workman's-compensation-type injuries. Should the loss of sight in an eye because of a surgical complication result in the insurance company's paying several hundred thousand dollars, whereas a similar injury occurring on-the-job results in an award of only one-fourth that? If a man's fractured leg does not heal well after an accident and he is left with a limp and discomfort, should the orthopedist's insurance coverage pay many multiples of what similar on-the-job related compensations would have been? A man's skin was discolored and thickened because of radiation therapy he received for a genital cancer. Although the cancer was cured, the gentleman was left with some skin disfigurement. A sympathetic jury awarded several hundred thousands of dollars in damages because of the radiation damage to the skin—yet the man's cancer was cured. A sympathetic jury was touched deeply by the sight of the skin changes—and equally untouched by the complete cure of the cancer! No malpractice existed; the skin change was a known possible complication of an acceptable plan for radiation therapy.

Another case in point is one in which a jury awarded over $1 million to a psychic who purportedly lost her powers after having a CAT scan. I find it a curious fact that this lady's cryptic powers were worth far more once lost than they could ever have been worth in reality! How absolutely absurd! Such examples abound under the present legal system. What an insult to society's integrity. Any system allowing such an outrageous outcome is so decadent it begs revision. Even though this decision was ultimately reversed, the fact that it ever happened in the first place is ridiculous.

Jury awards can involve far too much emotion. Some order of magnitude in jury awards is necessary to give order to the chaos. Better yet, a board or panel created for the said purpose of evaluating injuries and determining an equitable reimbursement would surely be an improvement. After all, if I were the injured party, I would like to think that a fair settlement would be made rather than having me go to a roulette wheel to "dial my fate." This system of award by chance exists only because the dollar amounts are based on the whims of a jury that is subject to the arguments presented by lawyers who have a vested interest in the case. The very thought of a lawyer encouraging his client to be sure to "look pathetic" so as to influence the jury is despicable. Awards and settlements should be determined by knowledgeable people familiar with an established set of standards. Anyone who opposes such panels identifies himself as having selfish, personal goals which exceed those of his peers. The establishment of such a board or panel would ensure equitable treatment for all injured patients, not just those with megabuck potential. The lottery concept and windfall decisions are contrary to a rational system of reparation for injury. Malpractice does necessitate reparation for injury—but it should be a just compensation. Only someone with a vested interest in the case would favor the windfall or lottery concept over a reputable panel's evaluation.

Supporters for the contingency fee arrangement continually refer to the fact that were it not for a contingency fee, most people would not be able to afford legal counsel for medical malpractice claims. This is an interesting argument because, in actuality, just the opposite effect has occurred. Since lawyers work for a contingency fee rather than for a fee for services rendered (as do 99 percent of other professionals), the larger the award, the greater their remuneration. Human nature being what it is, which cases do you think receive the majority of attention? The sensational cases do—especially those for which juries might make tremendous awards and those in which it is difficult to disprove a cause and an effect for an injury (that is, obstetrics and neurosurgery).

Negligence for which no large monetary award would be forthcoming receives little or no attention—no matter how obvious the error. It is akin to suing someone with no assets—you cannot collect anything. So instead of really helping the "little man" have access to the legal system, a contingency fee system only does so *if* the case in point promises the possibility of a large settlement. Some very grave injustices in medical care occur on occasion, but if such a case will not bring "recoverable" damages, the doctor escapes reprimand since no lawyer is interested in the case. This too is an obvious failure in the system, because there *are* some grievous errors that deserve strong censure; yet these fiascos escape notice if no money can be made from their occurrence. Surely, a knowledgeable panel could impartially review *all* cases involving "negligence" without regard to which ones might bring a "windfall." This would be to the delight of the vast majority of the medical profession: It would be a way to evaluate objectively any questionable practice by using a panel of qualified, true experts who have no personal gain in such proceedings. This would also be to the delight of the many reputable attorneys who have the proper humanitarian interest of truly improving medical care rather than looking to personal monetary gain. Medical societies and associations could fund such panels, and this would certainly be a welcome relief over the present system. Such a medical tribunal would have quality medical care as its aim—not personal income as the motivating factor. Such panels should include the clergy, business people, lawyers, and doctors—none of who should have any personal interest in the particular case being decided.

Under the present system of contingency fees, winning means everything. If you don't win, you receive nothing. Also, if an attorney "discovers" a case wherein an error in judgment was made and an injury resulted (for example, a baby developed cererbral palsy), it usually means instant big bucks. This may even happen with a minimum of legal work or simply by settling out of court. Properly selected, such cases are a plaintiff attorney's dream. Because such lucrative cases may require only a small amount of time because an error is obvious, is there any doubt which cases receive the most attention? There is little regard for the actual merit of a malpractice suit—the size of a possible award is the motivating factor. If I were in real estate, I would surely try to sell big, expensive houses that would require little time and effort to sell rather than tiny, inexpensive ones that might require lots of time and effort and generate only small commissions.

One further analogy in reference to contingency fees needs to be drawn. It is a known fact that almost one-third of all physicians—almost daily—either do or do not do something that could result in a lawsuit's being filed. This does not mean that negligence was involved—only that the physician's actions *could* possibly result in a suit under the present system. Furthermore, this does not imply that any injury occurred—simply that the "top gun" might have done something different. This does not imply that bad medicine was practiced or that harm was done—only that there is a constant vulnerability to lawsuit. A similar culpability exists for you as you drive your car every day. For instance, is there *any* day during which you do not break the law, at least by the legal definition of the traffic code? Do you stop fully at every stop sign—stop completely as defined by law? Do you speed up at caution lights and sometimes "run" a few? And, understandably, when you accelerate, don't you often exceed the speed limit (break the law) even though only momentarily? Have you ever "run" a red light after being in a turning lane because you were actually out in the intersection? This usually involves breaking the law, by definition. If we were to go strictly by legal definitions, all of us would be guilty of numerous traffic infractions every day.

Allow me to take this one step further. Suppose we put the police ("traffic cops") on a contingency basis—that is, 35 percent of the proceeds of their tickets would go into their own pockets. Can you imagine how many tickets would be written? And for how many minor infractions? The system could not function. Everyone would constantly be getting tickets. Almost one-third of all drivers would qualify for a ticket on a daily basis—either for something they did or did not do. A contingency fee for such policemen would create havoc. The anxiety created might just take the joy out of driving.

A means of settling lawsuits in a timely manner is definitely needed. It usually requires several years to resolve cases, and those that ultimately go to a jury trial require an average of two to five years to litigate. It is almost inhumane to stress the involved physicians for such a protracted period of time. Furthermore, a medically oriented arbitration board or panel could quickly eliminate frivolous suits. Conversely, such an unbiased tribunal could also help to establish the facts in legitimate cases. This would allow an objective evaluation of the situation rather than a subjective one. This is but another benefit of such panels. We desperately need to identify bad doctors, and the panels could certainly function in this capacity.

Returning now to juries and the problems they face, I can relate to the sympathy a jury expresses. Being compassionate, I, too, have great empathy for the injured patient. Let me emphasize again that doctors themselves are totally in favor of awards to injured parties—if substandard care *caused* the injury.

This is the very essence of malpractice insurance. Let there be no doubt that physicians desire reparation in indicated instances. Reparation however, should be commensurate with the injury. Being inspired and influenced by the visible evidence of an injury might allow an emotional jury to be unduly manipulated by a counselor. Reactions can sometimes resemble mob hysteria or the herd instinct when, unwittingly, people become emotionally charged and sometimes irrational. Again, this contributes to what has become almost a lottery system of awards rather than a system based on valid relative values. An evaluation by a well-trained *knowledgeable* board, experienced in medical injuries and physical rehabilitation, etc., could better determine what "pain and suffering" are worth in monetary terms. This task is difficult enough for professionals, but to expect an inexperienced, untrained lay jury to do this is unfair and terribly unrealistic. This designated board should be composed of both medical and legal experts (having no personal interest in the case), along with ministers, business people, and other respected leaders in the community.

It is relatively easy for personalities and emotions to enter into the jury's deliberations and decisions. Lawyers are quick to recognize that jury selection is so very critical to the outcome of a trial. After all, lawyers try to "mold" the jury during the trial, so they must pick people they feel are most easily influenced. A nationally prominent Florida plaintiff lawyer summarized things rather succinctly: "When you pick a good jury, the case is 90 percent won." According to an article in the *Wall Street Journal,* this lawyer won eight individual settlements or verdicts in 1986 alone, each one worth in excess of a million dollars! As his contingency fee, he demands, and gets, 40 to 45 percent of each award. His words in the same article, testify to his motives and his view of doctors: "I enjoy suing the bastards."[5]

The article also refers to a case where this same attorney represented a model who had lost her leg. In this malpractice case, he stripped her down to her shorts, and with the leg "hanging there," he argued her case. The jury awarded $3.4 million. Another ploy he uses is exemplified in a case involving the death of an eight-year-old girl killed by a truck. He put the girl's younger sister—a lovely blond child of seven—on the witness stand and had her read a poem she had composed about how much she missed her deceased sister. This clever lawyer has won in excess of 25 different multi-million-dollar settlements.

The adversarial relationship permeates the legal profession as dominantly as ethics does medicine. It is easy to understand the difficulty these professions encounter operating in the same arena. A tactic that lawyers typically use in a courtroom is one requesting yes or no answers. Medicine is an art and a science, and oftentimes many parameters greatly influence the situation, so a simple yes or no answer is *not* applicable. Physicians must be constantly on guard against being led by the plaintiff attorney. Many medical decisions involve qualifications and do not lend themselves to simple positive or negative statements. Oftentimes the physician is forced to use his "best reasonable judgment." Besides this, there are numerous instances of different approaches to the same problem by even the best of experts. It is unrealistic to attempt to evaluate science (medicine) by legal definitions, especially as regards the causation of injury.

Another example of injustice in the present system of jurisprudence is the fact that while the insurance company may pay some huge settlement, a negligent physician may come away relatively unscathed. In cases where truly poor medicine caused an injury, a monetary award might be made though the "wrong" perpetrated receives little or no attention. The guilty doctor may not even receive a reprimand. This disturbs competent physicians greatly. What do you think happens every time good physicians attempt to investigate an unethical or incompetent doctor? The physician in question has his lawyer inform the investigating body that such action is libelous. How can we "police our own" with the constant threat of legal repercussion? Obviously, arbitration panels could be created to handle this aspect of the system. If plaintiff lawyers were sincerely interested in the quality of medicine (rather than dollars), shouldn't the system address the problem of bad medicine rather than simply address the settlement in terms of monetary retribution alone?

Another injustice in the current system deserves mention. Large settlements are ultimately funded by the patient population at large. The scenario goes something like this: (1) large awards by sympathetic juries cost insurance companies money; (2) the insurance companies then raise their premiums to cover claims; and (3) physicians then raise their fees to cover the escalating premiums. So it is ultimately patients in general who actually finance this economic bonanza for the lawyers. Only a very small number of patients receive much money in this system. If a jury—charged with emotion and perhaps even partly out of contempt—decides that a "wealthy physician" should pay the injured party a large sum of money, this money ultimately comes from other patients. The physician comes away relatively unscathed from a monetary standpoint, unless it is an unusual case involving an inordinately large award which exceeds his coverage. Unfortunately, obstetrical liability—more frequently than for most other specialties—exceeds insurance coverage.

Obstetrics presents a rather unique jeopardy for the physician. The vast majority of neurologically damaged infants DO NOT exist as a result of anything related to labor and delivery. It is estimated by the leading authority in this area that only between 3 to 18 percent of such compromised infants result from circumstances related to labor and delivery.[6] It has been well documented recently that the majority of these infants' injuries antedated the delivery. In other words, the die was cast in advance of the delivery process. This is extremely difficult to "prove" in court, though, and, as stated earlier, the burden of proof is on the physician to establish his or her innocence. Furthermore, a compassionate jury only sees a pathetic child or situation and often feels obligated to help them. Who can argue with charity? But is this "charity" the obligation of the medical profession? This in itself represents a big problem today. The medical professional can ill-afford to finance catastrophic insurance to injured parties in the absence of malpractice. Such insurance may indeed be a societal responsibility, but this must be distinguished from medical malpractice. To accuse a sincere physician—innocent of malpractice, but the victim of circumstance—of substandard medicine is a very grave injustice. The accusation creates endless anguish for the physician. This intense anxiety —absolutely undeserved in the absence of negligence—is the single most important factor in obstetrican's abandonment of their practice. The anxiety over, and the vulnerability to lawsuit for a neurologically impaired infant to whom he has done no harm, is a greater burden than most physicians can bear. Once again, where good medicine is not sufficient defense against lawsuit, one is rendered defenseless. This then becomes an untenable situation.

Abuse of the Tort Law System

Any discussion of the major problems in the current system of medical jurisprudence would not be complete without mentioning the theory of the "deep pocket." This refers to the present use of the statute regarding "joint and several liability," a legal doctrine whereby each individual defendant is responsible for the entire amount of damages awarded, irrespective of that individual's involvement in the case. Simply stated, it means that the defendant with the greatest insurance coverage or most money will, in all likelihood, be responsible for paying the greatest share of any economic damages awarded. This is absolutely independent of the significance or degree of one's involvement in the case in question. That one is involved at all means that he shares total responsibility. Under such an arrangement, the one with the "deepest pockets" usually pays the most.

A statute that is equally ridiculous is the provision preventing disclosure of collateral payments to the injured plaintiff for injury. If this principle applied to routine surgery, a patient with several insurance policies could make a good profit just from having surgery. Shared liability is reasonable, but a person's liability should reflect his or her degree of involvement in the case. For instance, physician A seeks physician B's assistance during a very difficult operation. Physician B leaves the operating room after the difficult part of the operation, and physician A then forgets a sponge in the patient at the end of the operation. Physician B is then named as a co-defendant in the resultant suit —even though he was only responding to another physician in trouble during a difficult operation. I was named a defendant in a suit against an obstetrician because I assisted him during a difficult delivery (and all I did was to hold the infant's feet up for my partner to perform a breech delivery)—yet I was as responsible (economically) as he was for the entire delivery. Worse yet, a third obstetrician was similarly named as a co-defendant, and his total involvement in the patient's care consisted of the initial pelvic exam in the office when she was examined in early labor.

This kind of litigation is not just oppressive to medicine. A man purchases a lawn mower, for example. He may drink three beers and then carelesssly mow the grass and cut off his toe. He can sue the merchant. In this particular example, though, the manufacturer of the product in all likelihood will be the one with the deep pocket and may well be the party ultimately held liable.

In another example, a man who left a tavern somewhat inebriated mounted his motorcycle and shortly thereafter crashed into a car while the motorcycle was clearly on the wrong side of the highway. The cyclist then sued the motorcycle manufacturer and won an award in excess of $1 million. The jury, according to "60 minutes," was sympathetic because of the burns suffered by the cyclist when the vehicle caught fire after the crash. The liability was determined because of a faulty design of the motorcycle which allowed it to leak gasoline after a crash. What this means is that any merchant who sells a product risks his entire business with the sale of each and every item. Worse yet, he may be risking his personal savings should the customer have an accident, even though the customer is clearly at fault. This is despite a customer's carelessness, state of intoxication, stupidity, or disregard for instruction. And because of this "deep pocket" theory—more properly, joint and several liability—the manufacturer may be entirely responsible if his pockets contain the most money.

The entire subject of liability has been abused. Parents in a Florida trailer park were forced to remove their own swing sets from their "front yards" because the trailer park owner was held liable for an injury which occurred on his land (that is, in the trailer park). Swimming pools at hotels and motels no longer have diving boards because of liability. Playgrounds have removed the majority of gym equipment because of liability. A school board of education was held liable for injuries sustained by a burglar who fell through a skylight in the school. The tobacco industry is held liable for damages caused by cigarettes, yet what consumer is not aware of the possible health hazard of smoking? The legal community has extended the definition of liability too far, just as tickets for minor traffic infractions could be carried to extremes.

It is our duty as a responsible society to recognize that business transactions involve the exchange of assets. This is true whether it involves animal skins for frontier supplies or presently money for groceries. Today the buyer has a distinct advantage over the seller because of this extended liability. Product liability is now a factor in almost every transaction. Just as having a vested interest in writing traffic tickets might cause some traffic officers to issue citations for minor infractions, the legal profession has encouraged suit via this extended liberal interpretation of liability. It has become a source of tremendous income. It is no coincidence that trial lawyers are so vehemently opposed to any changes in the statutes governing medical/legal jurisprudence. Legislating any changes in the system (that is, tort law reform) will be extremely difficult since most legislatures are composed of many attorneys.

What is necessary at this point is an insurance policy against whatever contrived liability the buyer might desire. Basically, this would involve acquiring insurance as part of the purchase price of a commodity—not insurance financed entirely by the seller. If someone buys a lawn mower, for example, included in the price would be "insurance" to cover cutting off his toe should he use the equipment carelessly. This should not be at the seller's expense. If such liability insurance is desired, let it be a part of the purchase price. Given a choice between much higher prices for commodities with foolish kinds of insurance attached, or cheaper prices without such absurd amenities, I dare say the choice would be quite obvious.

If you smoke or abuse alcohol, you should include in the purchase price of each cigarette or drink an insurance against any perceived harm, rather than ransom the company producing the product. A drink should cost twice as much at a club or restaurant before its members or owners should be held legally responsible should the inebriated person have an automobile accident. The medical profession cannot be liable for every outcome that is not perfect. In the absence of negligence, physicians should not be forced to compensate patients for results that are less than desired in any case, much less in every case. If such monetary compensation is considered desirable, let the purchase price (the surgical fee or the delivery fee) include this—we should not merely extend the liability of the "seller."

When this extended liability becomes too oppressive, we begin to diminish the numbers of sellers. The buyer and the seller must be equals—especially if the patient-physician contract is to be honored mutually. The physician promises to do his best, and the patient accepts whatever reasonable risks are involved. If additional insurance is desired, it should be made a part of the purchase price. The seller already carries insurance against gross negligence—but not in the absence of clear *causation*. It is only fair that the purchaser (buyer) finance any additional insurance he may desire.

NOTES

1. Pearse, W. H., Professional Liability: Epidemiology and Demography. Clin Obstet Gynecol. 1988; 31:148.
2. Roberts, D. K., Shane, J. A., Roberts, M. L., eds. Confronting the malpractice crisis: guidelines for the obstetrician-gynecologist. Kansas City: Eagle Press, 1985; 13.
3. Gallup Poll, Princeton, N.J., 1985
4. Lebow, M.A., America's Schizophrenia: Public Understanding of the Malpractice Question. Clin. Obstet. Gynecol., 1988; 31:222.
5. *Wall Street Journal*, "Doctors' Nemesis; Florida Lawyer Wins Big Malpractice Suits, And Loves Doing It," January 11, 1988.
6. *American Medical News*, "Cerebral palsy—liability link low, but suits high," January 8, 1988; 48.

CHAPTER 6

Society's Role in Resolving the Crisis

MY OBJECTIVES in writing this book have included two goals. The first was explaining to my previous obstetrical patients why I felt compelled to discontinue the practice of obstetrics. The second was to emphasize to the public that a crisis in medical jurisprudence exists, and that their personal medical care is in jeopardy. I feel that it is imperative that a solution be proposed to alter this exodus from obstetrics. As you now know, the liability crisis includes all health care providers, and a proposal for obstetrics would be all-inclusive for medicine in general. This provision, it is hoped, would apply to the pharmaceutical industry as well, because extended product liability has certainly adversely affected recent advances, vaccines being the prime example.

It is somewhat ironic that the specialty most affected by the liability crisis should be such a "happy" one. That very fact, however, does help to explain why so many obstetricians are sued. Because obstetrics usually involves wellness care and healthy babies, it is easy to understand the tremendous disappointment over any imperfect result. Furthermore, imperfect outcomes in this specialty often involve a grave condition, specifically, cerebral palsy or the neurologically impaired infant. It is understandable that this malresult often generates anger, and the animosity is then intensified by the expense of caring for the child. Such anger helps to explain the astounding number of lawsuits against obstetricians. Seventy-three percent of obstetricians have been sued at least once,[1] and as an obstetrician, you can expect eight suits during your career, each lasting two to five years before settlement of the case.[2] You could easily spend your entire career either being sued, recovering from the ravages of a suit, or preparing for the next one!

The liability in obstetrics exists because of grave outcomes, large medical bills, and disappointment; but the reason that obstetricians are so terribly oppressed and concerned is because of the excessive magnitude of the awards. Surprisingly, claims result in payment in 46 percent of the cases filed in obstetrics.[3] This also means constant anxiety for the obstetrician regarding the possibility of exceeding his liability coverage. And when he considers that he is involved in lawsuits for such a considerable part of his life, it is no wonder that the stress becomes intolerable to many obstetricians.

I am extremely concerned about the future of obstetrics but, more importantly, about medicine in general. It has been therapeutic for me to write this book because I have vented some frustration. Yes, although I have quit obstetrics, I have only just begun to fight for it! Obstetrics represents the prime target in the medical tort law system because of the megabuck awards, but all of medicine will benefit from proper liability reform. This translates as better care, not only for society but also for you as an individual. I truly hope that you, the reader, now understand the serious ramifications of this liability crisis!

The solution is actually ridiculously simple. It does *not* lie primarily in tort law reform. The solution lies in guaranteeing fair payment for injury caused by physician negligence. That means adequate, not excessive, compensation to anyone whose injury is *caused* by physician negligence. It does not mean that the physician is responsible for payment for maloccurrences unless substandard medical care was provided. By all means we should keep the tort system. As a part of the tort system, we shall continue to employ the legal counsel so necessary to run this complex process. We desperately need attorneys to officiate legal matters. The attorneys, however, must work on the basis of a "fee for services rendered," just like the rest of the work force in this country. The potential for excessively large incomes from contingency fees in malpractice cases encourages plaintiff attorneys to initiate suits whenever there is a malresult, but oftentimes in the absence of negligence. It is human nature to want to aid victims of tragedy. I support the American Red Cross, both emotionally and financially, but the jury is not the Red Cross, and it is not their duty to compensate patients in the absence of physician malpractice. Because the practice of medicine is both an art and a science, a jury's challenge to identify negligence and establish causation is made even more difficult.

Two things must be remembered. First, Monday morning quarterbacking is always easier; hindsight is always 20/20. Second, judgment calls in medicine are often based on many factors, in addition to which human error must be considered. For instance, a pitcher throws the third strike. Let us say that the umpire misses the close call. If the ump followed the ball from the time it left the pitcher's hand until it crossed the plate, and it was above the batter's knees but below his chest, and the ump used his best reasonable judgment to make a close call, then there is no negligence on his part. If he did not watch the ball, or did not consider all of the factors (waist high, over the plate, whether the batter swung the bat), then he might be guilty of negligence. One further point in this baseball analogy is worthy of mention. Whether the umpire observed the ball crossing the plate or not involves both art and science—art because the angle at which the ball was observed could influence the umpire's perception, and science because the ball had to have gone measurably over the plate. This judgment call must be accepted by anyone who plays the game. The umpire is *accountable* for his call, but he cannot be held *responsible* for the batter's strikeout, because he exercised his best reasonable judgment. He might have erred; but he was not negligent.

Not to belabor the point, but another word of caution is necessary regarding causation in medical malpractice and product liability. Medical treatment, based on one's best reasonable judgment, frequently involves choosing between conflicting theories or approaches. There are many established, though different and acceptable ways of performing operations, managing infections, diagnosing disease, etc. The jury's job as "triers of fact" is to determine *causation,* and this also frequently involves choosing between conflicting theories. The defendant's attorney and the plaintiff's attorney both try to present their theory in conclusive terms to convince the lay jury. Frequently, there is a limitation of available data, and as new knowledge becomes available, a "correct" decision made in 1980 could be "incorrect" by the standard of 1982! This is further complicated because experts present opposing conclusions with the same set of data! This forces a jury to make a finite decision regarding causation when, in actuality, there may be none. The jury is charged with the definite endpoint of making a final decision, yet conclusive evidence may be lacking for either the plaintiff or the defendant.

Certain legal precedents have tremendous implications for medicine and pharmaceutical companies. It is accepted, for example, that juries and/or judges can make decisions regarding causation when there is scientific evidence that causation has been shown to be unlikely in large populations. In a case involving Ortho Pharmaceutical Corporation, a judge ruled that a vaginal contraceptive gel used by a lady *caused* birth defects in a child conceived during the use of the contraceptive. There was substantial evidence presented during the trial which showed that in large populations the incidence of birth defects was no higher when the contraceptive gel was used than when it was not used. The judge elected to conclude that in the case of this particular child it was more likely than not that the gel did cause the defect. The appellate court's decision to uphold the causation was based upon the appellate court judge's opinion that, "Plaintiff's burden of proving that Ms. X's child's defects were caused by the product did not necessarily require them to produce scientific studies showing a statistically significant association between spermicides and congenital malformations in large populations." The appellate court determined further: "It does not matter in terms of deciding the case that the medical community might require more research and evidence before conclusively resolving the question."[4]

It is dangerous when the court uses a "more likely than not" philosophy in making decisions regarding individuals, rather than looking at the scientific data regarding the effects on large populations. This gets back to the same problem: In medicine physicians are considered *guilty* until proved *innocent!* What will it take to show the world that the tort system employs an adversarial process wherein each "camp" presents the medical issues as either black or white, attempting to convince the jury regarding causation? A better question might be: Who should be held responsible for compensating the injured patient, especially in the absence of definite, identifiable causation? I strongly urge that we eliminate tort liability that is predicated on a societal "need" to compensate the injured party. In the absence of wrongdoing, misconduct, or lack of established causation, a defendant should not be expected to compensate a plaintiff.

If the principal theme in the solution to the liability crisis is the proper and fair compensation to the deserving, injured party, let us devise a system wherein the injured patient receives the greatest share of the money paid. Surely we can improve upon a system wherein only 28 cents of each malpractice insurance dollar ends up in the hands of the injured plaintiff.[5] It has been reasonably well established that 95 percent of the claims *paid* originate from indefensible, negligent medical care.[6] The negligence is quite obvious. Therefore, let us establish a Medical Malpractice Review Board, a board which could make a timely review of medical malpractice cases and establish not only culpability but also the equitable monetary reparation for such alleged injuries. This would automatically eliminate 70 percent of the legal expenses involved in litigating medical malpractice cases. Furthermore, a medical peer review board could readily identify the 95 percent of cases in which obvious negligence occurred and was indefensible,[6] thereby allowing 63 percent (95 percent of cases times 70 percent of dollars) more money to be paid to the injured patient rather than to the adjudication process. This would at least provide a system wherein 90 percent of the money rather than 28 percent went to the plaintiff! This could be done without altering the present tort law system at all. If the vast majority of meritorious suits were managed this way, it would provide the quick resolution necessary for handling the increasing number of tort cases. In 1985, there were 78,000 tort cases in the state of New Jersey![6] In the United States, in 1986, there were 43.7 suits filed per 100 obstetricians! Now, you can understand why it normally requires two to five years to resolve the average medical malpractice suit. Perhaps the United States does need to graduate 40,000 lawyers per year.

The Medical Malpractice Review Boards being proposed should be composed of physicians, business people, ministers, and other representative lay people. There should be enough physicians on the panel to evaluate the medical care properly—that is, to determine the alleged negligence actually *caused* the injury. These medical experts will have no vested interest in the award in any case. Their job is to interpret facts in the case to establish if negligence was the cause of the injury. They should be paid for the time they spend in interpreting facts —not for their advocacy for the plaintiff or the defendant.

A distinct advantage that such a review board would offer is proper assessment of the compensation for injury. Knowledgeable business people could evaluate logically what the cost of care for injuries would be, what earning potential had been lost, and the monetary value for loss of limb, etc. They could also determine how to structure a settlement so that the injured party received equitable payment every year, no matter how long or short their illness might be. They could even include a provision for inflation, annuity payments, or whatever good business people would deem best for that individual. In a local malpractice settlement, $450,000 went to the plaintiff's attorney at the conclusion of the litigation, and the parents of the compromised child were to receive only $48,000 per year for ten years. If we look at this closely, the attorney could invest this money, and if he got a return of 10 percent on his investment, he would be earning $45,000 per year—almost as much as the plaintiff would be getting, without eroding the $450,000 principal! What a mockery of justice for the attorney to receive more than the plaintiff!

Another wonderful advantage of a Medical Malpractice Review Board would be the ability to identify truly negligent behavior by physicians and to work jointly with the State Medical Licensing Bureau in monitoring the quality of medical care. This would satisfy the desperate need to "police our own." Let well-trained clinical physicians evaluate medicine—be it for negligence or for quality of care.

Thus far, by setting up a Medical Malpractice Review Board, the tort law system has remained unaltered. Cases would simply go to a review board first. The accomplishments, however, would be great. They would include settling the 95 percent of grievous errors quickly and unceremoniously while allowing equitable compensation to injured patients as determined by qualified persons. At the same time, it could identify doctors not measuring up to the standards of care and establish a way for these physicians to be monitored or censured by the

State Medical Licensing Board. This is certainly not accomplished by the present tort law system, but it would be very beneficial.

The establishment of a Medical Malpractice Review Board could also simultaneously address two specific abuses of the present tort system. The first is the exposure of collateral sources of income which a plaintiff may have, such as another responsible party previously having agreed to a large settlement. Again, equitable compensation is desired—not a system whereby an injured party exploits the insurance company for personal gain. The second is the excessive awards for exemplary damages and for "pain and suffering." A limitation or "cap" could be set for this type of damage—possibily not to exceed $100,000. This cap on *unpredictable* awards by emotional juries removes the physician from personal financial liability if he carries reasonable insurance coverage. In the present situation, even with the excessive premiums paid by the physician for malpractice insurance, there is the possibility that he could easily be sued for millions of dollars over his coverage. Few, if any, physicians could afford premiums to cover such damages. Besides, it is well known in the medical community that the more insurance coverage you have, the more likely you are to be sued by a young, aggressive plaintiff attorney.

If attorneys so strongly support maintaining the provision for unlimited ceilings on awards for pain and suffering, let us consider the following proposal. The argument behind pain and suffering and punitive damages is reparation for the mental or psychological damage the injury caused the plaintiff. If this is true, then in those instances where the jury or medical malpractice board found that the defendant doctor was not negligent, the physician should be entitled to equal punitive or pain-and-suffering compensation. The misery of a suit should not be borne by the physician alone if he is innocent. Considering what some plaintiffs and their attorneys assess as the monetary value of pain and suffering, I shudder to think of the lawyer's liability in having to compensate the physician for the pain and suffering which resulted from a frivolous or nonmeritorious suit. But turn about *is* fair play.

It is known that most malpractice grievances are settled in favor of the defendant doctor. I interpret from this that numerous non-

93

meritorious cases are filed by angry patients, many of whom may have legitimate complaints regarding physicians' indifference and lack of communication. Obviously, this lack of communication and indifference by physicians causes the initiation of many more malpractice cases than does true negligence. Although this type of grievance is not deserving of monetary compensation, it certainly has an adverse effect on the perception of the medical care being provided. Let there be no doubt that good physicians deplore such insensitivity by other doctors. Such *suboptimal* care by an indifferent or insensitive physician could easily be addressed by a Medical Malpractice Review Board. Censure is definitely in order; monetary compensation is probably not.

Let us now consider that remaining 5 percent of cases involving malpractice, but in which the medicine practiced was possibly defensible. These cases, in all probability, involve judgment decisions and will be somewhat controversial. They may require a more extensive review of the material and facts concerning the alleged injury. This could be performed initially by the Medical Malpractice Review Board, and once the validity and complexity of a case are identified, it could then be referred to the usual tort system if either party so desires. Being evaluated initially by impartial medical experts with no vested interest in the case is still advantageous to all of the parties involved.

A plan for establishing a Medical Malpractice Review Board at the state level has been proposed by the American Medical Association. The principal feature of the plan involves the creation of an expert medical peer review panel similar to that previously described in the preceding paragraphs. The plan would even provide attorney assistance at no cost to the claimant. If the initial claims review did feel the suit was meritorious, it would suggest appropriate settlement. Likewise, if the suit was determined to have no merit and there was no physician negligence, the board would call for dismissal. If the initial review was contested by either the defendant doctor or the plaintiff, it could be further investigated, with the expense being borne by whoever wants to precede with the litigation. This would allow ease of access to a further, more extensive review, a second opinion, so to speak.

There are tremendous immediate benefits from such a system. Claims could be processed quickly and at significantly reduced expense. A much higher percentage of the award would go directly to the plaintiff. Physician performance, especially in reference to the three E's (economics, education, and ethics) could be monitored more closely. Not controlled—*monitored!* Fairer compensation to injured patients would stablize escalating malpractice insurance cost and eliminate the patient population at large from financing a lottery system. The greatest advantage to physicians would be rapid distinction between meritorious and nonmeritorious claims while eliminating the incapacitating anxiety regarding a crippling windfall judgment, frivolous suits, and persecution by "hired guns."

The problem of medical liability is extremely complex, and it is certainly not likely to disappear. Because of its complexity, there is no "quick fix" to its resolution. Society feels that for every real or perceived injury (1) there must be someone responsible, and (2) there must be compensation for the injury. Let us remember, however, that causation is the prerequiste for responsibility and monetary awards. In the absence of a definable cause, this debt should not be assigned to the physician.

Just as society desperately needed the Good Samaritan Act, society now needs something to curb the increasing number of medical malpractice suits. Before the passage of the Good Samaritan Act, physicians and paramedical personnel were being held liable for giving aid at accidents, disasters, and other emergencies. Needless to say, society suffered the consequences as these needed health care providers withheld their services because of the fear of liability. There is a frightening parallel here. Health care providers are once again seeking ways to avoid liability. Medical school applications have declined, both in quantity and quality. Good physicians are seeking early retirement; high-risk services are being curtailed. Once again, society needs a new Good Samaritan Act—one which limits liability to truly negligent practice and accepts best reasonable judgment as adequate defense against malpractice.

95

NOTES

1. White, K. C., Professional Liability: Etiology," Clin. Obstet. Gynecol., 1988; 31:145.
2. American College of Obstetricians and Gynecologists. Litigation Assistant. Washington, D.C.: ACOG. 1986; 1.
3. *Ob. Gyn. News,* "Current Malpractice Insurance Crisis in Obstetrics Said to be One of Availability as Well as Affordability," March 15, 1988; 24.
4. Scialli, A. R., Causation in Science and the Law. Women's Wellness. 1988; 2:7.
5. Pearse, W. H., Professional Liability: Epidemiology and Demography. Clin. Obstet. Gynecol. 1988; 31:148.
6. Todd, J. S., Malpractice: Issues and Solutions. Audio-Digest Obstet & Gynecol., February 4, 1986.